TEACHING POLITICAL SCIENCE

TEACHING
POLITICAL SCIENCE:
THE PROFESSOR
AND THE POLITY

Edited by

VERNON VAN DYKE
Department of Political Science
University of Iowa

HUMANITIES PRESS INC.

Atlantic Highlands, N.J.

Library of Congress Cataloging in Publication Data
Main entry under title:

TEACHING POLITICAL SCIENCE

TEACHING POLITICAL SCIENCE
1. Political science—Study and teaching.
I. Van Dyke, Vernon, 1912-
JA86.P56   320'.07   76-54677
ISBN 0-391-00685-1

Printed in the United States of America

TABLE OF CONTENTS

Introduction

This book is addressed primarily to teachers and students of political science. It concerns a problem common to them all: how to make teaching better. The title suggests the framework of the inquiry: *The Professor and the Polity*. Students in political science classes are members of a polity—presumably interested members, and actual or potential participants. They thus have needs, and it is natural to suppose that the teacher should respond somehow to those needs.

The question concerns the kind of response. What objectives should the teacher of political science pursue relating to the actual or prospective role of students as participants in, or observers of, politics?

The dominant traditional answer has been Weberian: that the teacher should teach empirical knowledge and give minimal attention, if any, to moral issues; he should teach as objectively as possible, granting that he lacks a scientific basis for choice between conflicting values and that in most cases he also lacks a reliable basis for giving policy advice. Though teaching about government and politics, he should in the classroom be nonpolitical. Detachment should prevail even in the teaching of political theory and philosophy.

The traditional answer is under attack and has been for some time, overlapping criticisms and suggestions being made. Some say that the teaching of political science is itself unavoidably a political act, necessarily reflecting philosophical and ideological presuppositions and having political implications and consequences. This means that the teacher cannot prevent his values and policy preferences from influencing his teaching, and that he should admit it and make the influence deliberate. Whether or not accepting this view, some adopt the old proposition that the teaching of political science should include training for citizenship, and give the proposition an interpretation that calls for attention to both the empirical and the moral ramifications of political policies and issues; American critics in this group tend to be supportive of the American democratic system and to believe it both proper and desirable to lend support to that system in the classroom. Some critics take the view that the teacher should have the promotion of justice as his goal, tutoring the students in its requirements.

vii

The problem is not a new one, but most of the attacks on it have related primarily to research. The concern here is with teaching, and presumably this makes a difference. The researcher, if he chooses, can select and formulate his problems with a view to engaging in scientific inquiry; and especially when he focuses on relatively narrow problems the influence of his values may be difficult to determine. The teacher in the undergraduate classroom, in contrast, must deal with relatively broad problems, handled in the world of politics on the basis of judgment and moral choice; and whether the teacher can, or should try to, keep his own values from influencing what he does is a question. Of course, the researcher may reject an exclusive commitment to science and take up moral problems, but the teacher may have no practical choice.

To restate and elaborate on the above, the problem of improving teaching and making it responsive to the needs of students can be discussed in various terms:

1. It can be discussed in terms of the question of deliberately promoting purposes ranging from the supportive to the subversive. Should the teacher seek to inculcate attitudes favorable to the political order? Should he seek to be neutral? Should he seek to promote ameliorative change? Revolution? Should the answer be the same regardless of the nature of the political order within which the teacher works? Should it be the same regardless of the issues that are current and regardless of the degree of public tension and crisis? Should it be the same regardless of the composition of the classes taught—the same in relation to all students whether or not they equally enjoy their civil, political, and other human rights? Is it incumbent upon teachers to urge students to participate in political and governmental affairs in order to bring about change?

2. Essentially the same questions can be taken up from a slightly different perspective. What should be the role of the teacher with respect to scientific and moral questions, respectively? Are elucidation and explanation the sole legitimate purposes in the classroom? Should the door be open also to some or all kinds of evaluation? Is evaluation an essential aspect of undergraduate teaching? Is it the main purpose of teaching to put the student in a better position to take appropriate moral and rational considerations into account in making political judgments and choices? Should the aim be not simply to provide the student with a basis for moral and rational judgment, but deliberately to steer him toward judgments that the teacher approves? Whatever the answer to these questions, what should the relative em-

phasis be on detachment and reflection, on the one hand, and commitment and activism, on the other?

3. The questions posed above can, with some reformulation, be directed at public policies. The policies can be put into two categories: (1) those relating to or affecting the political system itself, and (2) those designed to have effects outside the system—for example, on private persons or on foreign governments. Should the teaching of political science at the undergraduate level be concerned with public policies in either or both of these categories? Should the concern simply be for the process by which policy decisions are made, or should it also be for the content and probable consequences of policies? Is the answer the same with respect to both foreign and domestic policies? Should the emphasis and the purposes of the teacher differ depending on whether he is dealing with the domestic and foreign policies of the United States, or with the domestic and foreign policies of other countries, or with policies developed at the international level? What should be the relative emphasis on the problems of the United States and the problems of mankind?

These questions, formulated in collaboration with Martin Diamond and Stanley Rothman, were put to a group of political scientists selected for the known diversity of their views and for their prominence in the field. Responding to the questions, they prepared papers that were first discussed at a Benjamin F. Shambaugh Conference at the University of Iowa in October, 1974. The conference was supported not only from the Shambaugh fund but also by the National Endowment for the Humanities, and it was arranged in cooperation with the Division of Educational Affairs in the national office of the American Political Science Association. In addition to the authors of the papers, members of the various committees of the APSA having to do with education participated in the conference. The papers, some of the them in revised form, are presented in this book with a view to stimulating thought and discussion throughout the profession.

VERNON VAN DYKE

TEACHING POLITICAL SCIENCE

CHAPTER 1

Mainstream Political Science and Its Discontents

STANLEY ROTHMAN
Smith College

In the purple rhetoric of a Manchu prince of the time (1644): "Our . . . humane and merciful armies [are] rescuing the people from the water and the fire, bringing peace." The Manchus were saving China from itself and its own excesses.

Much of this was mere propaganda. In fact, . . . the Manchus had (long before) set their cap for conquest, and their repeated raids across the Great Wall had done much to create the problems the Ch'ing now claimed to solve. It was their presence in the North, for example, that had forced the Ming to levy additional taxes and drive the peasantry to arms.

Frederick Wakeman, Jr., "High Ch'ing: 1683-1839," in James B. Crowley, ed., *Modern East Asia: Essays in Interpretation* (New York: Harcourt, Brace & World, 1970), p. 3.

Although the fervor, the direct confrontation politics, and even the violence of the 1960s have all but disappeared from American campuses for the time being, it is clear that the events of that period have left their mark on the academic community. This is especially true in the social sciences which, in many cases, bore the brunt of student demands for immediate "relevance," and whose practitioners, in probably larger numbers than in other disciplines, sympathized with many of the goals of the student activists if not always their methods.

The 1960s critique of the American university and those who taught within it by both radical students and their academic counterparts claimed that far from being the ivory tower it pretended to be, the university was part of the "system of oppression" which they were fighting. The activities undertaken by universities, indeed the very categories used by professors of social science to deal with "reality," served to reenforce the "system" rather than confront it truthfully and produce meaningful change. The "objectivity" claimed by social scientists, especially so called "behavioral scientists," was a cover for reifying the present and ignoring the possibility of "liberation."

The renewed emphasis by political scientists in the 1970s on deal-

1

ing with policy questions and moral issues can clearly be traced back to the challenges posed by the previous decade, as can the renewed concern with undergraduate teaching. The "New Left" in political science had succeeded, with the aid of students, in compelling a re-examination of "mainstream political science" to an extent far greater than had been true of earlier criticisms of dominant trends, most notably that of Leo Strauss and those influenced by him.[1] Just as importantly the new awareness by political scientists that the manner in which the profession is organized and the way in which political science is taught both have significant social and political implications for the larger society is a direct result, I think, of the ferment of the past decade, although other factors have not been without importance.

I am convinced that political scientists of earlier decades failed to concern themselves seriously with the possible impact of their teaching and writing upon the larger society for two reasons primarily: (1) Intellectuals generally felt that they lacked real prestige or power in American society and that what they did had relatively little effect on the "real" world. (2) With some exceptions political science and the other social sciences were characterized by an unselfconscious consensus as to the "nature" of American society and of reality in general. It was a "liberal" consensus which, by and large, accepted democratic institutions of the American variety as natural and good for civilized persons, and was dedicated to reforming these institutions so as to make them more liberal. Whatever one's theoretical views of the relationship between facts and values, most of us (and I include myself) felt that intelligent people naturally supported Adlai Stevenson and the views associated with him, and we pointed with pride to the fact that our brighter students tended to be "liberal democrats," a fact we attributed, laughingly, to their greater intelligence and perceptivity.

During that period the "Left" was weak and relatively discredited. The major critique of the consensus just described aside from those of a few "traditional" American conservatives within the profession, and members of the non-academic community who saw the university as a hotbed of radicalism, came from Leo Strauss and his students. It was their argument not only that American political science was characterized by serious errors, but that the ideas held and propagated by political scientists were seriously damaging to the health of the polity.

By and large complaints from the larger community were ignored by most academics. Those making them were regarded as "yahoos" and worse, who were not to be taken seriously except where their activities threatened to impinge upon academic freedom. Leo Strauss himself had an immediate and powerful impact at the University of Chicago, and indirectly upon a somewhat larger number of political scientists, but I think it fair to say that his influence within the profession as a whole was minimal.

To suggest that the New Left has forced a re-examination of the prevailing mood in political science is not to say that either it or the Straussian critics of mainstream political science are correct. We can only deal with that issue and its relationship to both research and teaching after we have examined the received position and those of the critics in somewhat more detail. This examination will constitute most of the remainder of my paper. Along the way I shall not hesitate to criticize the arguments I will be summarizing, and in the end I will offer a brief statement of my own position on some of the issues under consideration.

From a theoretical perspective the issues which have stimulated the most controversy between students of Strauss and members of the New Left on the one hand, and mainstream political scientists on the other have been those relating to the nature of political knowledge. Is the study of politics a science in the same sense that the term is applied to physics? If not, does the attempt to follow a "scientific model" lead to conservatism (the Left), or to a weakening of civilized values (students of Strauss)? And what is the relationship between purely descriptive and ethical statements? Are they analytically separate, or in the social sciences at least, do they flow from (or depend upon) each other?

At a conference on the TEACHER and the polity, it may seem rather odd to devote an entire paper to such old chestnuts, but, on reflection, it makes eminently good sense. For, aside from relatively narrow questions of technique, what we teach and how we teach our discipline are very much tied in with our view of it, as we shall see when we examine the writings of both the critics and defenders of mainstream political science. To be sure, our view of our appropriate classroom role is also affected by our view of the nature of the political system in which we live and the problems it faces. But these substantive issues themselves are not unrelated to theoretical controversies of the kind noted above.

I

I think it fair to say that the dominant view within mainstream political science as regards the nature of political knowledge during the 1950s and early 1960s was heavily influenced (although perhaps in a watered down and second hand version) by "positivist" analyses of the nature of science. The position is familiar to all of us. The primary job of the social scientist is to understand reality. While we can, perhaps, never achieve full objectivity in such matters, our efforts should be, as much as possible, directed to that end. Further, facts and values belong to separate realms of discourse and can not be derived from each other. Moral statements are merely statements of personal preference. This is not to say that social scientists have nothing to say about ultimate value issues. They can, as Weber suggested, clarify the structure of arguments and indicate the consequences of proposed courses of action. They cannot, however, decide scientifically that one basic value position is superior to another. Heinz Eulau's discussion of these issues in *The Behavioral Persuasion in Politics* exemplifies the position nicely.[2]

This stance was not uniquely that of "behaviorists." After all such views were held as well by scholars like George Sabine who can hardly be called part of the behavioral persuasion, and there have always been individuals who are classified by some, at least, as behaviorists in orientation who held to rather different positions. For example, it is quite clear that Gabriel Almond owes more to the instrumentalism of John Dewey in his thinking about the relationship between political science and ethical problems than he does or did to positivist orientations, narrowly defined. His secular political culture (obviously a preferred type) takes its values from an examination of the "facts" and changes them as requirements demand.[3] Almond and others, in fact, have been criticized (I believe wrongly) for suggesting that we should change some of our "values" because the "facts" do not support them.[4]

However, it is true that most mainstream political scientists have not been terribly interested in moral questions professionally and that, by and large, their teaching emphasis has been upon trying to help students to understand "reality" better, through the analysis of reality. I suspect, too, that most of them would agree with Weber's argument that in the classroom they should remain, on the whole, as objective and fair as possible and should concentrate on description and on empirical, as against ethical, propositions. Whether they have succeeded in doing so, or indeed can succeed in doing so, is another matter.

Leo Strauss certainly felt that they had not and, indeed, could not succeed in such a venture, for facts and values are inextricably interwoven, and those who have followed in his footsteps continue to take much the same position. To Strauss and his students the attempt to separate facts and values has simply allowed contemporary political scientists (when their work is not meaningless) to introduce unexamined value premises through the back door as it were. And these unexamined premises, in addition to being erroneous, have proven quite dangerous.[5]

Four assumptions of contemporary social science have particularly disturbed students of Strauss. The first is the unwillingness of the modern mind to accept the idea that there is a natural order in which man finds his place and which serves as a guide to appropriate moral behavior. In their view man has a nature which can be discovered; and, thus, a full description of any human situation in its significant aspects automatically entails an ethical judgment about it. Moral judgments are a species of factual judgment and are subject to rational discussion and examination. The second is the tendency of modern "liberal" social scientists to view problems of a moral nature in terms of the satisfaction of individual wants or desires. While not opposed to considering such wants or desires, the classic view, which is accepted by Straussians, is "perfectionist." Moral dilemmas revolve about determining policies which are designed to enable human beings to perfect those excellences which represent the essence of man's nature, to the degree which it is possible for given individuals in given circumstances. This may, in fact, mean denying that expressed wants or "needs" always provide moral imperatives. Third, those accepting the classical position reject the "radical" egalitarianism which they see as characteristic of the modern temperament, considering it destructive of a healthy democratic polity. They also reject the modern version of "perfectibility" based on the assumption that the conquest of nature is desirable and/or possible and, if successful, will resolve most of our moral dilemmas. Finally, they are skeptical of the notion that it is possible to create an ideal community which will achieve that end. The Platonic model remains an "idea" which may serve as a guide but which will never be achieved.

To Strauss the source of these contemporary assumptions lies in a philosophic tradition that began with Machiavelli and was transformed by Hobbes, Locke, and Rousseau into modern Liberalism. With additional accretions derived from Marx, Nietzsche, Weber, and others, such assumptions constitute the unexamined premises of much of contemporary social science. Thus contemporary social science is based on a "vulgarized" version of Liberalism; vulgarized because its practitioners are unaware of the origins of the tradition and of the arguments upon which it was founded.

In this form contemporary American mainstream social science emphasizes the lack of human limitations and refuses to make judgments about the worthwhileness of various forms of human activity. In the view of students of Strauss, mainstream political science (although it does not recognize the fact) is partly responsible for the current social malaise and the attack on all forms of rational discourse. This is true not only for the reasons cited above but also because mainstream political scientists tend to engage in uncovering the sources of the myths underlying the polity, and to debunk them. There are, in Strauss' view, things better left unsaid (or stated with a "non-corroding" caution) in a polity which at least partially incorporates the principles of justice.

If I understand him correctly Strauss always felt that in teaching the young it was far more important to help them develop their latent philosophical understanding of these key issues, rather than to fill them with supposed facts about the world or highly abstract theories of social process, which they could not directly relate to their own experience.

Strauss' critique of contemporary social science in the United States would, if true, constitute a powerful indictment. However, I would be prepared to argue that those adhering to the classical tradition have yet to demonstrate that their view of "reality" is more plausible than that accepted by contemporary social scientists. In this regard I have very little to add to criticisms of Strauss which I have developed elsewhere, although I will return to some of the issues involved after describing the New Left critique of contemporary social science.[6] I am more impressed by Strauss than I once was, and far less sure of my own position, but I remain skeptical of his basic argument. The classical position was closely bound up with classical natural philosophy. It is not supported by our current understandings of the natural world. Any tenable philosophic position must, it seems to me, be built on those understandings.[7]

II

The critique of "mainstream" political science (and social science in general) by the "New Left" also questions many of its assumptions, although Straussians have argued that in some ways the critique (or at least parts of it) can be seen as a natural extension of the liberal perspective, which explains, in their eyes, why so many liberals feel "defensive" when confronted with that critique.

Radicals argue that the supposed liberalism of the university has been a kind of "corporate" liberalism, supporting a state which seeks to defuse the demands of the young and the disadvantaged by minimum social reforms. Social scientists have behaved in this way partly because they have sold out to corporate interests and the power elite, and partly because of the framework of assumptions within which the discipline conducts both research and teaching.[8]

Their counter is to urge political scientists to identify with those in the society whom they consider downtrodden and exploited, and to work actively to radically change the system. If most political scientists during the 1940s and 1950s accepted the general parameters of the system, many of those identified with the New Left view contemporary America as almost absolutely evil or, in milder terms, as a madhouse, as these quotes from those among the more restrained members of the group I am so identifying indicate:

> . . . [T]he world shows increasing signs of coming apart; our political systems are sputtering, our communication networks invaded by cacophony. American society has reached a point where its cities are uninhabitable, its youth disaffected, its races at war with each other, and its hope, its treasure, and the lives of its young men dribbled away in interminable foreign ventures. Our whole world threatens to become anomalous.[9]

. . . .

In so far as the new utopianism [i.e., behavioralism] elim-
inates alternative realities by embracing as "real" the very
institutions which the social sciences properly subject to continuous criticism, it is anti-empirical as well as elitist. When
it fails to acknowledge the problematic—not to say grotesque
—character of the present it is unable to specify how men are
kept underdeveloped by the dominant order of commitments:
government by a plurality of elites, a functional division of
labor . . . the system of fixed social and biological roles within hierarchical organizations . . .[10]

To some who have identified themselves with a more radical
perspective, the problem with mainstream political science lies less in
the philosophic bases upon which it rests than in a failure of its practitioners to examine evidence carefully and to use their imagination.
Thus one finds critiques levelled against such scholars as Robert Dahl,
Bernard Berelson and Gabriel Almond among others for assuming
that the American model of polyarchy with relatively low political
participation (from the point of view of the critics) represents the
best we can do. Evidence is presented to suggest that the present
system may operate the way in which it does because of weaknesses;
that these weaknesses are corrigible, and that the classic "model" of
democracy which emphasizes full participation by all citizens can be
realized if we are willing to change the system in certain basic ways.
Indeed the classic liberal model must be implemented if the citizens
of the polity are to attain full moral self-development.[11]

Generalizing from this position, Sheldon Wolin suggests that the
problem lies somewhat deeper. Operating within the framework of
a restrictive paradigm describing the political system, political scientists, he claims, have tended to reify its assumptions even at the moment of its collapse. Instead, he suggests, they should be advancing
new possibilities on the basis of "critical" theory.

Relying upon Thomas Kuhn's *Structure of Scientific Revolutions*,[12] Wolin suggests that, indeed, this method has historically been
that of the natural sciences. The natural sciences operate on the basis
of paradigms which contain "normative" elements. Revolutions in
science occur when the old paradigms can no longer solve key problems, i.e., when they result in anomalies. It is then that new paradigms
are introduced which (again) contain normative elements that serve
as a guide to "normal" science, i.e., ordinary empirical research. What

is good enough for the natural sciences should certainly be good enough for the social sciences. And so:

> The issue is not between theories which are normative and those which are not; nor is it between those political scientists who are theoretical and those who are not. Rather it is between those who would restrict the "reach" of theory by dwelling on facts which are selected by what are assumed to be the functional requisites of the existing paradigm, and those who believe that it is . . . the task of the theoretical imagination to restate new possibilities.[13]

The moral decay of our present society demands that we find new paradigms solving the problems which beset us. And, it is clear from this text that to Wolin these paradigms necessarily rest on a "moral" vision.

Christian Bay would agree. Real as against pseudo politics is concerned only:

> . . . with that activity aimed at improving conditions for the satisfaction of human needs and demands in a given society or community according to some universalistic scheme of priorities, implicit or explicit.[14]

In contrast:

> Pseudopolitical refers to activity that resembles political activity but is exclusively concerned with promoting public or private interest group advantage, deterred by no articulate or disinterested conception of what would be just or fair to other groups.[15]

To Bay justice is knowable, as indeed it was for the authors of the classics. Unlike the classical formulation, however, Bay conceives of justice as knowable to most if not all men, and his view of justice is based on the assumption, ultimately, that it is possible to create a society which will satisfy the real needs of all (relatively equal persons) as they perceive these needs. Bay would, therefore, emphasize the teaching of justice and the reorganization of political science teaching and research to concentrate on methods of achieving it.[16]

Bay is not unique in this regard. Many if not most of those who subscribe to the "New Left" critique of mainstream political science stress the moral dimension. To them the ends are given. They know the evils of the system. The goal of teaching and research is not to understand the system or to develop propositions about it which can be used by evil men, but to concentrate on finding ways to change it fundamentally. Thus Lewis Lipsitz makes his commitments quite explicit and urges that both research and teaching concentrate on ways of promoting "intellectual liberation." Students would study "the inequities and oppressiveness generated by many existing structures and processes. . . ." They would explore how they "re-structure the allegiance of poor whites in the South" and assess the possibilities for a "new party of the left" in America.[17]

From a rather different perspective the same stance has been taken by a number of other social scientists. The argument is that objectivity in the social sciences is ontologically impossible; that one's work is necessarily embedded in a value frame and that the best one can do is to understand the source of one's values, and clarify them. Since values permeate social research, empirical analysis will differ widely depending upon the value frame from which one starts. It was this theme which David Easton picked up in his presidential address on the "post-behavioral" revolution.[18]

Interestingly enough few if any American political scientists have developed this position in systematic detail, although it has been much brooded about. The main arguments have come from sociology where Alvin Gouldner's oft cited volume, *The Coming Crisis in Western Sociology*, takes a position very much like the one all too briefly summarized above.[19] Gouldner explicitly calls for a social science which orients itself to "liberating" mankind, at the same time that he calls upon social scientists to examine and clarify the sources of their own value orientations. He is convinced that new possibilities can only be realized through *praxis*, i.e., through using research and teaching to create new realities. A social science which limits itself to describing reality "objectively" is *ipso facto* guilty of reifying the present and supporting its repressiveness.

Gouldner's position finds some support in the writing of political scientists like Henry Kariel, whose latest emphasis, however, seems less focused upon direct attempts to restructure the social order, than upon using the classroom experience itself to liberate both students and teachers. To Kariel politics involves just those areas where limits can be challenged, and it is the function of the teacher to encourage his or her students to challenge limits wherever possible. To become aware of the possibility of "expanding the political present" or opening previously closed systems, is to become aware of politics. Teaching then takes on the practical characteristics of group therapy in which students and teachers join in awakening new possibilities in themselves. Process become more important than content.[20]

III

Those who suggest that "objectivity" in our research or in the classroom is impossible because value assumptions permeate all our theories seem to me nihilistic in the extreme. If such is the case our analyses or suggestions for change are of no greater value than those of someone who suggests that the road to salvation lies in the drinking of carrot juice. More practically, if such arguments were correct, state legislators would have every reason to suggest that they have as much right to determine the content of courses as do teachers of political science. Indeed, the profession would be defenseless against anyone who urged that, given the "liberal" bias of most political scientists, quotas should be set to insure that every social science department give equal representation to each political point of view. Fortunately, most of those who urge the "value laden" position theoretically, do not act as if they believe what they say. For the most part they write and teach as if their grasp of present realities and future possibilities is superior to that of their students or state legislators precisely because they have a better understanding of the manner in which the social world actually functions.

Indeed most of the propositions that they label value judgments and that supposedly determine the direction of our work, are essentially beliefs about such present realities and future possibilities. This is as it should be. If a social scientist or anyone else were unwilling to defend his or her arguments as regards the "oppressive nature of monopoly capitalism" or the possibilities of "liberation" by reference to "facts" about the present world, and the human beings who inhabit it, most of us would refuse to take him or her seriously.

Let us imagine a political scientist urging the desire for "equality" as a basic value underlying his work, an assertion that some on the left have made when arguing that their values differ from those of main-stream political science. Let us imagine further that this person was faced with the "factual" claim that attempts to achieve full equality would necessarily fail and would inevitably lead to an increase in human misery. Do we honestly believe that it would be reasonable to reply, under such circumstances, that this was, after all, a value question that might influence what we consider to be facts, but that neither the value position nor the facts were subject to evidential considerations?

Some of the issues most hotly in dispute among political scientists may not lend themselves easily to "ultimate" proof or disproof because of the nature of our discipline, because of the universe we inhabit, or because our beliefs satisfy deep psychological needs.[21] This is not, it seems to me, a reasonable argument for failing to chip away at them as best we can and for attempting to bring to bear upon them the best evidence we can muster. A position suggesting that we *merely* clarify our values is most often a rationalization by someone who does not wish to be disturbed by the facts.

Part of the difficulty in this area appears to stem from a series of category confusions. Political theorists often conflate the terms "normative," "value," and "moral" as if they were one and the same, but while *all* moral judgments are certainly value judgments and, in some sense are normative, we do not ordinarily consider the obverse to be true. When Thomas Kuhn, for example, argues that the facts scientists see are determined by "norms," he is not talking about moral judgments. Rather, he is suggesting that certain generalized conceptions of the nature of reality determine our perception of the "facts."[22] While it may be difficult to directly attack these normative bases of "ordinary" science, they are ultimately subject to factual checks. So, too, when it is asserted that underlying all science is a belief in the value of science, or, in a more limited way, the value of curing cancer, the assertion is generally a short hand way of suggesting that a certain procedure or type of research may have desirable consequences. Both statements assume that rational discussion and the bringing to bear upon these subjects of "objective" evidence is possible.[23]

The argument advanced by Wolin and others in their attack on Almond, Berelson, *et al.* appears equally dubious, despite Wolin's attempt to base it on Kuhn's work. As already indicated, Kuhn argues that theories change when anomalies are encountered while attempting to use such theories to solve puzzles. They are discarded only when new paradigms emerge which ultimately explain and predict events more satisfactorily, i.e., enable scientists to better solve puzzles.[24]

Now the theory which Wolin is attacking, at least as Almond presents it, is roughly as follows.[25] Contemporary democratic orders ("civic cultures") do not function the way in which civics texts describe them. That is they do not consist of the citizenry actively and rationally participating equally in making political decisions. On the contrary not only do citizens in successful democracies fail to behave in this way, but they can not. Indeed any approach to full participation in such a political order would lead to stasis, instability, and perhaps eventual collapse of the democratic polity.

British and American politics are relatively successful (these were the examples Almond was using) in part, because citizens also invest considerable emotional energy in their work, their families and their leisure activities. Participation in politics does not have great salience except at certain critical junctures. It is kept in its place.

Actually, Almond argues, the civic culture and stable democracy depend for their continued success on an uneasy balance between the myth of the rationalist activist citizen, the non-salience of politics, and the willingness of most citizens to behave as "subjects" most of the time. The rationalist activist myth is necessary so that citizens will "act" frequently enough to keep elites in line and so that elites will expect such action. If special groups of citizens act only at certain times and on issues which are salient to them, the polity can respond to their demands, thus re-enforcing their allegiance.

The balance, however, does face certain dangers. If issues of considerable salience to substantial segments of the population emerge and can not be dealt with in a reasonable time, serious problems can develop. Citizen activity can increase to a point where elites, caught up in all sorts of cross pressures, will be unable to act at all, and citizens whose demands are not met could develop a sense of impotence and alienation, with serious consequences for the system. Further, in so far as socialization into the civic culture stems less from early childhood experiences (although these are important) than from experience with the political process itself, the impact of a crisis like this on later generations could be fairly substantial.

Assuming the argument to be correct, its further implications are rather disturbing. Mass activism would probably result in either a

longish period of political stasis punctuated by considerable violence
or some sort of dictatorship. In the latter eventuality voluntary participation might be replaced by directed participation, but the great
mass of the population would, in fact, be merely subjects. Of course
some of the issues which brought about the crisis could be resolved
and political activity would then fall back to normal levels.

I've extended and extrapolated from Almond's argument somewhat for a particular purpose. It seems to me that it offers some interesting insights into the current malaise of American democracy,
especially among upper middle class youth, although among other
groups as well. Both the Vietnam War and the race issues generated
a series of conflicts involving upper middle class youth (and their parents) allied in some cases with blacks versus various middle and working class "ethnics." Despite all the rhetoric about power elites it seems
quite clear that upper middle class reformers failed to achieve their
aims not because of "elite" opposition (after all, they and their par-
rents constitute a substantial part of the social establishment at least,
if there is an establishment) but because a segment of the political and
social elite has joined with the working and lower middle class white
majority in opposition.[26]

Thus, the stasis and increased alienation from the "system" which
characterized American politics during the late 1960s and into the
1970s can be interpreted as the result of a conflict between a number
of politically mobilized groups, each expecting the system to respond
to what it considers legitimate demands, and each feeling that the
system is not responding.

It does not seem to me that there is anything in this argument
which "obscures" the facts by a paradigm, as Wolin suggests.[27] It
may be that Almond and others, in suggesting that mass activist participation (or participatory democracy) are not good things are confusing twentieth century Americans with mankind and that a broader
perspective is necessary. And it may be that their emphasis upon stable
democracy is exaggerated and that other values should be taken into
account (but who seriously would *opt* for instability *per se?*). However, neither the fact that the political system is in trouble (I'll ignore
Wolin's hyperbole), nor the fact that Almond and Verba's theory
contains what Charles Taylor has called a value slope which gives it,
in Wolin's mind, a "conservative" cast, is sufficient ground for rejecting it.

To reject it, Wolin and others would have either (a) to demonstrate that they can produce an alternate theory that explains the facts (contemporary politics) better and has a more "radical" value slope (in Charles Taylor's terms, *undermining* the theory), or (b) to suggest an alternate set of values that it is better to achieve, thus (to use Taylor again) *overriding the theory*.[28] Wolin attempts neither of these tasks. Reduced to its basics his argument for rejecting the theory rests merely on a dislike for its moral implications. His position parallels the Church's rejection of Galileo's theories of planetary motion, and has as little to commend it.

Walker's argument is rather similar. He is distressed by the attack of Almond, Berelson *et al.* upon classical democratic theory partly on moral grounds. Full democratic participation must be implemented because only with such participation can people develop their full moral potential. However, aside from the fact that he seems to have confused classical democratic theorists with 1940s civics texts, he offers little evidence for the assertion.[29] As Malcolm B. E. Smith has pointed out, it is not at all clear that political participation has these results, although the ability to participate may.[30] And, indeed, if Almond and Dahl are correct, *full* participation would have the opposite results whether we like it or not.

Reflecting on past human history and drawing one's views from the past and present condition of man may lead one to "conservative" views with respect to future programs. This is no excuse for rejecting such views for a *ouija* board. Marx, incidentally, would agree. The bitterness of his attack on the "Young Hegelians" who went about calling for socialism on the basis of their belief in the superiority of the idea of socialism is to be explained in these terms. In a particularly biting paragraph he suggested that their behavior resembled the actions of a man who wanted to fight the *idea* of gravity because it resulted in many drownings, as the statistics invariably demonstrated.[31] Marx, then, spent the remainder of his life attempting to demonstrate that socialism was probable, if not inevitable, by developing a theory which, he felt, explained the past and the present better than alternate paradigms, and thus could be used as a guide for the future.

Wolin seems not unaware of this, at least subconsciously. Criticizing behavioral political science, he cites Max Weber (who, he suggests, was a behavioralist or, rather, a philosopher of method) to point to the dangers of limiting oneself to narrowly based paradigms.

Weber, he argues, was aware that the contemporary bureaucratic world was leading to "a polar night of icy darkness and hardness. . . ." Actually, Weber uses the phrase to describe what will happen if, as he suspects, current radical agitation is followed by radical victory or a political reaction leading to chaos and disorder. In the same essay he condemns as "intellectual windbags" and false prophets those who set forth romantic images of future possibilities and refuse to relentlessly face "the hard realities of life."[32]

Hanna Pitkin makes the same point rather elegantly:

> . . . [T]he acceptance of reality is the only possible basis for genuine change, as the recognition of who we are and what we value, of where we are and what we face, of "our present commitments and responsibilities," is the only genuinely solid foundation for successful action and meaningful change. If you want to move purposefully, knowing where you are may seem to limit your alternatives, but it is also a prerequisite. Such knowledge is like friction. As Wittgenstein says, in our desire for absoluteness, for transcending the human condition, "we have got on to slippery ice where there is no friction and so in a certain sense the conditions are ideal, but also, just because of that, we are unable to walk. We want to walk; so we need *friction*. Back to the rough ground!" The desire to escape our human condition does come to each of us at times. It is a real desire, but not a desire for something real. It is a vain desire.[33]

I have spent a good deal of time on Wolin's essay because it is one of the few really serious statements of a coherent philosophic position by an American political scientist somewhat identified with the Left. The only other with which I am familiar (aside from a revival of Marxism among some younger scholars) involves an attempt to combine elements of Phenomenology, ordinary language philosophy, and selected ideas from what has come to be known as the Frankfurt school of sociology, popularly identified with Marcuse, Adorno, Habermas, and others. The limited writing in this area by political scientists seems to me rather more muddy than deep. However, one major and classic essay presenting something of this perspective deserves some consideration because of its clarity, and intellectual power. I refer to Charles Taylor's, "Interpretation and the Sciences of Man."[34]

Drawing heavily upon implications he sees deriving from all of these approaches, Taylor criticizes "mainstream political science" for its assumptions about the existence of "brute data," and the consequent requirement of verification. Because of these assumptions mainstream political science, according to Taylor, can not understand that our society, like all societies, is defined by intersubjective understandings which themselves constitute its reality. It is impossible then to really understand another society whose reality (i.e., common understanding) is different from ours: just as it is impossible to really understand our own without clarifying the meaning of the understandings which underpin it. Further, given the self-reflexive quality of human beings, i.e., changes in understanding lead to changes in identity, no real prediction is possible in the social sciences.

To replace the empiricism of mainstream political science, Taylor suggests a discipline based on "hermeneutics." Essentially, this involves an attempt to clarify the understandings which underpin our action by making coherent sense out of them. Intersubjective agreement is to be obtained not through reference to predicted empirical outcomes, but rather through constant attempts to clarify and make coherent the understandings which are the subject of controversy. In the last analysis continued disagreement can only be resolved by urging individuals who do not understand to more radically change themselves.[35] Thus, there can be no "value free" science of man, for changing oneself means to act according to new rules that include positive evaluations of certain ways of acting.

As an example of the inability of mainstream political science to understand societies other than our own, Taylor points out the difficulties of our really comprehending the traditional Japanese village which operated out of a powerful need for consensus rather than a bargaining mentality.

> Our whole notion of negotiation is bound up . . . with the distinct identity and autonomy of the parties; it is a very contractual notion. But other societies have no such conception. It is reported about the traditional Japanese village that the foundation of its social life was a powerful form of consensus, which put a high premium on unanimous decision. . . . Now the the difference between our society and one of the kind just described could not be well expressed if we said

we have a vocabulary to describe negotiation which they
lack.[36]
. . . .
The language is constitutive of the reality, is essential to its
being the kind of reality it is. To separate the two and distinguish them . . . is forever to miss the point.[37]

Mainstream political scientists like Lipset or Almond can not understand our own society, Taylor suggests, because their methods
prevent them from comprehending its underlying assumptions.

All industrial civilizations have required a huge wrench from
the traditional peasant populations on which they have been
imposed; for they require an entirely unprecedented level of
sustained monotonous effort, long hours unpunctuated by any
meaningful rhythm, such as that of seasons for festivals. In
the end this way of life can only be accepted when the idea
of making a living is endowed with more significance than
that of just avoiding starvation.
. . . [T]his civilization of work is only one aspect of modern
societies, along with the society based on negotiation and
willed relations. . . .[38]

I, for one, would concede a good deal to Taylor. At least some
mainstream (and radical) political scientists, in their search for underlying "real causes," have ignored the fact that our reality does consist,
in part, of inter-subjective understandings. I am also quite willing to
concede that because we are reflective beings these understandings
can and do change in ways that make it unlikely that we can hope to
develop a science of society comparable to some of the natural
sciences.[39]

But Taylor is making his case by setting up a straw man; i.e., by
assuming that mainstream political science consists only of the work
of some of its practitioners. After all much of what he has said is
fully compatible with the work of Weber and of many other social
scientists who consider themselves part of the mainstream, including
the belief that one can produce changes in "reality" by changing understandings of that "reality."

It is, however, difficult to accept Taylor's implication that these
understandings constitute the core of reality and the implication that
they can not at least be partly explained by reference to other kinds

of reality including objective economic conditions, resources, climate, *et cetera*, to which indeed, various kinds of understanding may constitute more or less adaptive responses. Here Pitkin's critique applies as well to Taylor as to Wolin. And indeed, Taylor's methodology would seriously impoverish (I would argue) our "understanding" of how and why rules differ and have differed among various social groups.

Indeed I am not sure what Taylor means by "understanding." To be sure, social scientists can never understand the constitutive rules of traditional Japanese villages in the way the Japanese understood them, and yet Smith's description of these rules, which Taylor accepts and uses, is an "understanding" based on European categories and is subject to the types of empirical checks that social scientists love, including predictions as to what kinds of behavior are likely to be manifest under certain social conditions.[40]

Similarly, his own description of certain aspects of the constitutive elements of European civilization is not foreign to mainstream social science and has been the subject of considerable debate. One finds it hard to understand how, indeed, one could come to accept Taylor's perspective (which resembles Weber's) as against equally cogent alternative reconstructions without relying upon some kinds of empirical tests, including the study of the values of various groups in transition from one kind of society to another. More importantly Taylor's description is on a very high level of abstraction. One wonders how he could conclude that "modernization" is "wrenching" to peasants by simply examining the understandings characteristic of peasant and capitalist societies. Surely such a proposition requires evidence other than a reconstruction of the rules underlying such understandings. Theoretically, one supposes, Taylor could identify with traditional peasant conceptions of such rules and thus "understand" the trauma of the transition. That kind of evidence, however, is always open to the charge that he was merely "slumming," and that his supposed identification with the peasants was a cover for some other motives unknown even to him.[41]

IV

Despite some nods in the direction of the Frankfurt school of Phenomenology, the writings of most of those "radicals" who criticize mainstream political science seem to rest less on the argument that a new approach is needed than upon a conviction that the political system is totally evil and that they (and all men and women of good will) must by their actions (including their teaching) seek to bring it down.

If one judges them by their research proposals rather than their philosophic stance, their methodological position and the problems they face differ less from the people they most criticize than they think. For example both Marvin Surkin and J. Peter Euben, on somewhat different grounds, chastise Heinz Eulau for his assertion that scientific knowledge about politics can be used by those whose values he does not share.[42] Eulau sees this as a dilemma, while Surkin and Euben maintain that the social scientist must take responsibility for the type of work he does so as to make sure it can not be used by the wrong people. However, neither of them offer any evidence that this is possible. Indeed, in so far as they claim that research should be oriented toward "humanistic" change and that their findings can be helpful in creating that change because they are valid, they are faced with the same dilemma that Eulau is. After all, theories designed to help the poor organize more effectively can be used just as readily by those who wish to prevent such organization.

Among those on the Left, Henry Kariel remains an exception to the above remarks. So far as I understand his position, he now rejects the possibility of any meaningful value commitment. Both his writing and his teaching, then, become a way of satisfying the self by doing interesting things which, to him, means encouraging students to expand the boundaries of the self by "letting go." I am less than fully persuaded by his arguments. Indeed I think that his teaching methods are potentially destructive. Most adolescents need help in strengthening ego boundaries, not support of the powerful forces within them which are striving to break through. Whatever one's feelings about the nature of our society, it has become evident, I think, that the emphasis on "doing it" which characterized the 1960s was quite destructive for substantial numbers of young people.

Some of the major differences between mainstream political science and its critics on the Left have involved matters of style and temperament. By and large mainstream political scientists have always emphasized the cognitive role of teaching, whether as with Eulau they felt that ethical matters, ultimately, were not the concern of the social scientist, *qua* social scientist, or as with Almond, they felt that in some not clearly defined way, social science contributed to the solution of moral problems. They have argued that the prime function of the political scientist at the university is to work as hard as possible to clarify the nature of political reality, and to explain why it is that way.

Students of Strauss, while they differ sharply from mainstream political science, share a commitment to the cognitive nature of the discipline. Values are felt to be interwoven with facts, but Straussians insist upon an intellectual analysis of the facts; moral judgments should be made in the classroom, but with care, and they should be based ultimately on a close analysis of reality. Straussians also share the view that the academy should not normally seek to foster ideological polemic or social activism.

A good many of the newer critics of mainstream political science reject these views, both on philosophic grounds and on the basis of their conviction that the existing political system is evil and the power of the "establishment" overwhelming. These feelings have led them to espouse direct action in the classroom and to the desire, not only to restructure the university but use it as a base for social action. A good deal of the momentum for this enterprise has temporarily dissipated, but one can see it emerging again under appropriate circumstances, for I doubt that the emotional commitment of the activists has changed.

At the same time there is, for some at least, a rejection of an emphasis on "academic" learning of a traditional kind in terms of a direct experience of which "street knowledge" is considered a useful paradigm. As Surkin points out in an article in *P.S.*, quoting Murray Kempton with approval:

> I think there is a change now in our view of life; we know more than we ever knew before, but we know it instinctively, and not from the sources of public information we get. What do we know exactly? We know now that Walt Whitman Rostow is a fool. We know that Dean Rusk is a clerk. We know that Mr. Nixon is not really very much worse than the people who preceded him. . . . We know all these things not because anyone told us but because events have explained them to us. And it is this explanation that people are looking for.[43]

Surkin's perspective is, he argues, derived from a phenomenological approach which he, and others, claim to find in some of the writing of the Frankfurt School. The emphasis on street knowledge, then, is part of a view of reality which involves taking *most* seriously knowledge uncontaminated by the theories of empirical political scientists. The emphasis on *praxis* is related to the belief that in action, ideas about new kinds of reality (new "values") create a new reality and are, thus, validated. The classroom, then, becomes a place for encouraging and organizing action by students.

In one sense the stance of political scientists such as Surkin resembles that of students of Strauss or less sophisticated conservatives (the "Yahoos"). The ideas which are propagated in the classroom can vitally affect "reality." But again if our description of reality is determined by our "values" why is the political scientist necessarily in a better position to make judgments about its nature than anyone else? And, indeed, why shouldn't state legislators or alumni insist that varying moral views be available to students according to some quota or other. Indeed at least one member (Michael Parenti) of the "New Left" has urged just this, criticizing for example, the *American Political Science Review* for not printing enough reviews by scholars on the "Left."[44] However, although Parenti suggests that more conservative views also be represented with some frequency, it seems fairly clear from the thrust of his essay, that he is not convinced that such views deserve as serious consideration as those of his own constituency.

V

Earlier I argued, as against Surkin, Euben, and others, for the autonomy of descriptive statements and the analytic distinction between moral and existential propositions. I also, however, argued for their mutual interdependence, urging that, in fact, our moral views are affected in very basic ways by our views of reality and, in fact, should be. I know of no more forceful recent statement of this position than that of Charles Taylor in his essay "Neutrality in Political Science":

> . . . "[G]ood" doesn't *mean* "conducive to the fulfillment of human wants needs or purposes"; but its use is unintelligible outside of any relationship to wants needs and purposes. . . . For if we abstract from this relation, then we cannot tell whether a man is using "good" to make a judgment, or sim-

ply to express some feeling; and it is an essential part of the meaning of the term that such a distinction can be made. . . . "[G]ood" is used in evaluating, commending, persuading and so on by a race of human beings who are such that through their needs, desires, and so on, they are not indifferent to the outcomes of the world process.

In setting out a given framework, a theorist is also setting out the gamut of possible politics and policies. But a *political* framework cannot fail to contain some, even implicit conception of human wants, needs and purposes. The context of this conception will determine the value-slope of the gamut. . . .

In this sense we can say that a given explanatory framework secretes a notion of the good, and a set of valuations, which cannot be done away with—though they can be overridden—unless we do away with the framework.[45]

The structure of the argument is, I believe, akin to what Marx had in mind.[46] And indeed, if one takes John Rawls' seminal work on justice, another modern attempt to deal with this issue, there can be little question but that our views of reality are closely connected with ultimate moral decisions.[47]

This is not to suggest that moral views never impinge upon the work of social scientists in ways that guide their research and make rational discussion of issues difficult. The argument over whether the United States was guilty of "genocide" in Vietnam is a case in point. The term "genocide" as characterized by Lemkin in 1944 means briefly, extermination of a national or racial group as a planned move. At least some of those who wish to apply it to Vietnam suggest that it be expanded to a result which flows knowingly from a war policy even if the policy is shaped by other objectives. William Connolly, in a very perceptive and important essay, from which the above discussion is taken, uses the example to argue for the *impossibility* of separating out factual and moral considerations and for the inevitable loading of the former by the latter.[48] But does the example make his point? Let us examine it more closely.

First, the question whether genocide was a *known consequence* of American military policy is essentially a factual question. (Two factual questions are actually involved.) Beyond that, it is clear that the attempt to broaden the definition is an effort to associate American policy in Vietnam with a set of historical events which those desirous of expanding the definition suspect most people will naturally regard as evil. Their desire to equate American policy in Vietnam with the extermination of the Jews and other groups by the Nazis certainly reflects their view that the war was unjust for a whole variety of reasons. But the effort itself is based on the assumption that the underlying values of most of these individuals who may presently disagree with them are *not* essentially different from theirs. Why else should they attempt the expansion?

Once this is admitted the debate shifts to direct arguments about the justice of American policy in Vietnam—arguments which, I suggest, have to do with the nature of the regimes in the North and South and estimates as to the costs and consequences of the policies the United States has followed. And I would maintain that, if the discussion could proceed far enough, one after another of the supposed differences in moral values would dissolve into "factual" questions, for both sides would maintain that the policy they support is ultimately the more humane one.

Obviously I am not suggesting that such dissolution makes the agreement on the issues involved any easier. Self interest and ideological commitments (especially when tied together), as well as all sorts of unconscious needs and biases, may prevent rational discussion. The point is that such discussion *is* logically possible and the assertions made are theoretically subject to some sort of empirical test.

Let me summarize the argument so far. While those attacking mainstream political science (both students of Strauss, and those on the Left) have made some telling points, they have not made their case. It is clear that attempts to model the social sciences narrowly in the image of say, physics, are likely to be less than fully successful. However, this does not mean that general "scientific" canons should not serve as a guide. These include, among others, the logical coherence of propositions, parsimony of explanation, and, most importantly, the necessity of stating propositions in a form which permits some sort of inter-subjective validation.

More important, for our purposes, the argument that moral values inevitably shape our work thus making "objective" factual descriptions impossible is simply wrong, and the assertion of it self-defeating. Moral and factual propositions are of a different order. It is possible to describe "objectively" without at the same time engaging in moral evaluation, and, indeed, one must be able to do so if one is to be able to engage in meaningful moral discourse.

What are the implications of this perspective for our teaching and our research? It seems to me that if those who are "discontented" are wrong, so was Max Weber and so are scholars like Eulau. We have more to offer our students (and the general public) than a clarification of alternative courses of action. We can offer them a kind of wisdom which may enable them to make better moral-political choices.

However, to maintain such a position is to place even greater responsibility on the social scientist to reflect carefully and dispassionately on the world than does Weber's view, for if we do, we must accept the fact that our "paradigms" and our "facts" contribute in key ways to our students' basic moral assumptions. Thus, this perspective places upon the teacher the burden of constantly re-examining his or her understanding of reality, and attempting to free himself as best he or she can from the emotional and cultural blinders which inhibit objectivity.[49] I am not arguing against moral commitment in the classroom or in the university as a whole but only against the creation of the kind of "moralistic" atmosphere which would hamper such careful and dispassionate reflection.

It is not my impression that mankind has ever lacked opportunities for revolutionary "praxis," or the applications of "instinctive" knowledge to political situations. Nor am I convinced that historically we have witnessed a dearth of testing limits as human beings have attempted to act out their fantasies. In our own society the university, with all its imperfections, is one of the few places which permit the possibility of disinterested reflection about the problems which beset us. By their very nature such opportunities are not generally available to the great mass of citizens. Most of the time most individuals are forced to confront life situations on the basis of more or less immediate reactions. Underlying the idea of the university is the conviction that the opportunity for such reflection, and the existence of institutions which encourage it are good things.

Of course, the conditions which are conducive to reflection tend to limit the capacity of the teacher to deal directly with practical issues; just as immersion in "praxis" limits the ability of the political leader to reflect on more basic matters. Some few may be able to partially bridge the gap; most can not. Every movement in one direction

reduces one's effectiveness in another. Each time a social scientist becomes involved in practical political affairs, whether as an adviser to
governments, or a leader of student activists, he or she loses something
of his capacity for disinterested, compassionate analysis. This is not an
argument for an absolute refusal to engage in such activity. It is a
caution.[50]

Further most of us should stick to our last. Like it or not, many
of the real issues we face as a human family or as a nation call for
expertise and reflection in areas where our competence is bound to
be limited. We are not trained psychologists, sociologists, economists
or philosophers. As a group we are not ordinarily competent to really
guide our students in a sophisticated way to an understanding of the
implications of all these disciplines upon questions they and we have
about the world. We must touch on them, but it should be done with
considerable diffidence.

Thus, at least some of the criticism directed against those political
scientists concerned with the conditions of stability and instability in
political systems has been misplaced. While issues of justice can not
be ignored in such matters, an examination of the conditions of stability has historically been one of the central concerns of political
philosophy and should continue to be. This is the key area in which
to display our competence, for without some order nothing is possible, including justice.

I am quite aware that what I have said will not persuade those
of my colleagues who see the existing political system as one of complete depravity, dominated by an establishment which determines the
role that the university plays; i.e., an essentially conservative role. Many
of them are convinced that unless action is taken immediately things
will simply give way.

It is obviously impossible to deal with that issue in a symposium
of this kind. Nor is it likely that studies demonstrating that academics,
including political scientists, are more liberal than the population at
large will convince those who feel that the liberal end of the continuum is merely "corporate" liberalism. I can only state that in my
opinion this view is wrong on the face of it.[51] In fact, I am increasingly drawn to the conclusion that part of the malaise experienced by
our students during the 1960s and even today has something to do
with the failure of the world to conform to the liberal assumptions
upon which they have been raised. (In short, I no longer think that

Strauss' diagnosis of some of the problems we face is entirely wrong, although I am not prepared to accept his alternative.)

It is, after all, no accident that student activism began in those elite universities with the greatest concentration of the most liberal academics.[52] Nor is it unreasonable to suggest that the increasingly liberal orientation of students at these institutions was in some way related to the atmosphere of the colleges they attended. In 1971 J. Anthony Lukas, then with *The New York Times*, published a volume entitled half-humorously, *Don't Shoot—We Are Your Children!*[53] He was suggesting that the behavior of young militants was a natural outgrowth of what they had been taught by their liberal parents and liberal teachers. To be sure the students lacked the patience of the older generation and engaged in tactics the older generation did not like. They also carried some of the ideas of their teachers to extremes, from the perspective of these teachers at least. However, their radicalism, for good or evil, was certainly based on the assumptions with which they had been instilled; and the fact that they were often angrier at their "liberal" mentors than at admitted conservatives is a measure of their sense of betrayal by what they saw as the failure of these mentors to live up to the standards that they had set.

In any event, it seems clear that the liberal orientation of the university and its professors has had an increasingly important impact upon American politics, given its effects on students in an era of mass higher education.

These effects, I suspect, are lasting ones, especially among elite members of the professions. In a highly complex society where the causal relations among events are difficult to perceive directly, one's views of reality are increasingly determined by an abstract set of conceptualizations which it is difficult to prove or disprove. This is especially true for middle and upper middle class professionals who are—or at least have been—living in a fairly protected environment. Of course the professoriate itself is influenced by the media, the courts *et cetera* in a reciprocal fashion. I would only suggest that universities have come to have an autochthonous influence of some importance.

Liberal academics now find themselves continuously on the defensive *vis-à-vis* the Left. Faced with new forms of personal expression in the form of communes or gay liberation, they have (whatever their aesthetic tastes) been forced to accept these as bona fide expressions of individuality. Faced with a situation in which conventional

methods of reform have in the short run been less than fully successful in satisfying the demands of newly aroused groups, they find it hard
to resist the charge that the *system* must be at fault and requires radical change. Faced with demands for increased equality and participation on the part of all groups, they find it hard to criticize the legitimacy of such demands, despite some reservations about possible implications for the system.[54]

By and large the American citizenry during the 1960s accepted
with remarkable tolerance actions they abhorred, organized by students who did not have to work at full-time jobs, and who could raid
the community and then withdraw to the sanctuary of the campus
with relatively little worry as regards possible retaliation. It could (or
might in the future, should the pattern re-emerge) go the other way,
with the university in this country becoming really politicized as part
of a public reaction to the actions of its members.

I am increasingly persuaded that those in the general population
who suspect that the deterioration of our social life is related in some
degree to the fact that the intellectual community (including academics) has been telling us for some years how rotten we really are,
are not entirely in error. The influence of one or another teacher is
unimportant, but when the loudest voices in the intellectual community are committed to exposing the falsity of the values which sustain
us, and documenting every wart on the body politic, it is not unreasonable to suspect that they may be helping to create the malaise they
claim to be documenting. Those who urge *praxis* as a way of understanding and contributing to political change should not find such a
view too outrageous. The possibility that I may be right places an
extra burden upon those of us who remain unconvinced that the collapse of the existing order will necessarily be followed by one that is
superior.[55]

Aside from sharp disagreement with me on substantive issues, I
suspect that many of those whom I have criticized will find my counsel of disinterested (but compassionate) search for truth rather cold
blooded and unsatisfying. They are probably correct in believing that
while reflection is often a powerful weapon in breaking the cake of
custom, it can leave those committed to it unable to act in the face
of the very serious crises of our time.

Weber was aware of this problem in his essay, "Science as a Vocation." Reading it one can not but be struck by certain parallels to

our present situation. Then, too, young people wanted prophecy and a guide to action rather than sustained analysis, for they saw the world crumbling around them. Weber rejected this role for the teacher, even though he shared many of the aspirations of the young. He felt, I think, as I do, in a period which is faced with problems of far greater magnitude than was his. It may be that hard reflection on "reality" will not save us. On the other hand, unless our actions are based on such reflection, we are surely doomed.

FOOTNOTES

1. Under the rubric "New Left" I am including all of those who levelled sharp criticisms against "mainstream political science" from a "radical" perspective. Leo Strauss influenced a great many people. To avoid repetition I will sometimes speak of Strauss' students or "Straussians." Neither the term New Left nor the term Straussian is used pejoratively. I recognize that I am applying the designation to people who differ considerably from each other on a wide number of issues. However, in a short paper there is no escaping this kind of abbreviation, and, as I hope to indicate, the terms are reasonably satisfactory for my purposes.

I am using the term "mainstream political science" rather than "behavioralism" because the latter term has become a rhetorical catchall, applied to at least four types of political scientists, depending upon what one is trying to prove. It sometimes seems to apply only to those who model political science after the natural sciences, emphasize technique, and are concerned only (or almost entirely) with things that can be counted. At other times the term is expanded to include all those who emphasize "social processes" rather than formal institutions. At still other times it is further expanded to include all those who believe in a fact value dichotomy and/or, while not adhering to a rigid "scientific" model, believe, broadly speaking, that social scientists should, wherever possible, exhibit logical coherence in their propositions, and test theories by reference to their explanatory capacity and the "facts." Very often the term is used broadly to include all four types of scholars, while examples of the "evils" of behavioralism are chosen only from the first. In fact both the Straussian and New Left critiques have been levelled against all of the types noted above.

2. Heinz Eulau, *The Behavioral Persuasion in Politics* (New York: Random House, 1963). For a general discussion of professional orientations see Albert Somit and Joseph Tanenhaus, *The Development of Political Science, From Burgess to Behavioralism* (Boston: Allyn and Bacon, 1967), and Ithiel de Sola Pool, ed., *Contemporary Political Science: Toward Empirical Theory* (New York: McGraw-Hill Book Company, 1967). Weber's position can be found in Edward A. Shils and Henry A. Finch, eds. and translators, *Max Weber on the Methodology of the Social Sciences* (Glencoe: Free Press, 1949), and in Weber's much better known essay, "Science as a Vocation," in H. H. Gerth and C. Wright Mills, eds. and translators, *From Max Weber: Essays in Sociology* (London: Oxford University Press, 1947), pp. 129-156.

3. See Gabriel Almond and G. Bingham Powell, *Comparative Politics: A Developmental Approach* (Boston: Little, Brown, 1966), pp. 50-63.

4. For example by Sheldon Wolin, Lane Davis, and Jack L. Walker. See Sheldon Wolin, "Political Science as a Vocation," *American Political Science Review*, LXIII (December, 1969), 1065-1082; and Charles A. McCoy and John Playford, eds., *Apolitical Politics, A Critique of Behavioralism* (New York: Crowell, 1967), pp. 185-219.

5. See, among other volumes by Strauss, *Natural Right and History* (Chicago: University of Chicago Press, 1953); *What is Political Philosophy?* (Glencoe: Free Press, 1959). See also Herbert Storing, ed., *Essays on the Scientific Study of Politics* (New York: Holt, Rinehart and Winston, 1962). For a collection of essays which combine the criticisms of Strauss, students of Voegelin, and radical critics of mainstream political science, see George J. Graham, Jr., and George W. Carey, eds., *The Post-Behavioral Era, Perspectives on Political Science* (New York: David McKay Company, 1972). See also Martin Diamond, "The Dependence of Fact Upon Value," *Interpretation*, 2/3 (Spring, 1972), 226-235.

6. Stanley Rothman, "The Revival of Classical Political Philosophy: A Critique," *American Political Science Review*, LVI (June, 1962), 341-352.

7. For a recent and, I think, unsuccessful attempt to deal with this issue, see Eugene F. Miller, "Positivism, Historicism and Political Inquiry," *American Political Science Review*, LXVI (September, 1972), 796-873. The cited pages include comments by David Braybrooke, Alexander Rosenberg, Richard Rudner, and Martin Landau).

8. Aside from the volumes already mentioned, see among others: Philip Green and Sanford Levinson, eds., *Power and Community, Dissenting Essays in Political Science* (New York: Random House, 1969); Marvin Surkin & Alan Wolfe, eds., *An End to Political Science, the Caucus Papers* (New York: Basic Books, 1970); Theodore Roszak, ed., *The Dissenting Academy* (New York: Pantheon Books, 1968); and Alvin Gouldner, *The Coming Crisis of Western Sociology* (New York: Basic Books, 1970).

9. Wolin, *loc. cit.*, p. 1081.

10. Henry Kariel, "Expanding the Political Present," *American Political Science Review*, LXIII (September, 1969), 769.

11. See the Walker essay cited in footnote 4.

12. Thomas S. Kuhn, *The Structure of Scientific Revolutions* (Chicago: University of Chicago Press, 1962).

13. Wolin, *loc. cit.*, p. 1082.

14. Christian Bay, "Politics and Pseudopolitics: A Critical Evaluation of Some Behavioral Literature," in McCoy and Playford, *op. cit.*, p. 15.

15. *Ibid.*

16. Christian Bay, "Thoughts on the Purposes of Political Science Education," in Graham and Carey, *op. cit.*, pp. 88-99.

17. Lewis Lipsitz, "Vulture, Mantis and Seal: Proposals for Political Scientists," in Graham and Carey, *op. cit.*, p. 187.

18. David Easton, "The New Revolution in Political Science," *American Political Science Review*, LXIII (December, 1969), 1051-1061.

19. Cited in footnote 8.

20. Henry S. Kariel, *Saving Appearances. The Reestablishment of Political Science* (North Scituate, Mass.: Duxbury Press, 1972).

21. See the excellent recent discussion by W. G. Runciman, *A Critique of Max Weber's Philosophy of Social Science* (Cambridge: University Press, 1972).

22. Thomas Kuhn, *The Structure of Scientific Revolutions* (2d ed., en-

larged; Chicago: University of Chicago Press, 1970). J. Peter Euben's discussion of Kuhn is fairly typical of those who make this error. See his "Political Science and Political Silence," in Green and Levinson, *op. cit.*, pp. 3-58.

23. Runciman, *op. cit.*

24. Kuhn (2d ed.), *op. cit.*, pp. 174-210. As Kuhn makes clear in the second edition of his work, he regards the natural sciences as cumulative for just this reason. Unfortunately his attempt to clarify his work in the second edition takes much of the edge off his original formulation. Indeed, he specifically criticizes those in the social sciences and other fields who have interpreted his work as an argument for "relativism" in dealing with scientific theory.

25. The argument of the next few paragraphs is an abbreviated and slightly modified version of a section of my essay "Functionalism and Its Critics: An Analysis of the Writings of Gabriel Almond," *Political Science Reviewer*, 1 (Fall, 1971), 236-276.

26. See Walter Dean Burnham, *Critical Elections and the Mainsprings of American Politics* (New York: Norton, 1970), pp. 135-174.

27. Indeed a number of "radical" political scientists have been using essentially the same methods as were used by Almond and Berelson in an attempt to disprove their contentions.

28. See Charles Taylor, "Neutrality in Political Science," in Peter Laslett and W. G. Runciman, eds., *Philosophy, Politics, and Society*, 3rd series (Oxford: Blackwell, 1967), pp. 25-57. Euben, *loc. cit.*, and Walker, *loc. cit.*, along with a number of other critics of mainstream political science have relied, in part, upon Taylor's essay to develop an argument that denies the possibility of "objectivity" in the social sciences. I read Taylor quite differently. To me at least the essay suggests that we must strive even harder to develop better empirical theories if our value judgments are to be adequate, for the latter depend upon the former. I will develop this point more fully toward the end of this essay. It is only fair to note, however, that Taylor seems to have shifted his position somewhat. See his "Interpretation and the Sciences of Man," in *Review of Metaphysics*, 25 (September, 1971), 3-51. Incidentally, the term "mainstream political science" is borrowed from that essay.

29. Walker, *loc. cit.* To be fair, Walker also attempts to demonstrate that that approach of Almond *et al.* prevents us from perceiving certain aspects of reality.

30. "The Value of Participation," in J. Roland Pennock and John W. Chapman, eds., *Participation in Politics* (New York: Lieber-Atherton, 1975), pp. 126-135.

31. Karl Marx and Friedrich Engels, *The German Ideology*, ed. by R. Pascal (New York: International Publishers, 1947), p. 2.

32. Max Weber, "Politics as a Vocation," in Gerth and Mills, *op. cit.*, pp. 126-128.

33. Hanna Fenichel Pitkin, *Wittgenstein and Justice* (Berkeley: University of California Press, 1972), p. 339.

34. *Loc. cit.*

35. *Ibid.*, p. 48.

36. *Ibid.*, p. 23.

37. *Ibid.*, p. 24.

38. *Ibid.*, p. 39.

39. See Stanley Rothman, *European Society and Politics* (Indianapolis: Bobbs-Merrill, 1970), pp. 11-13.

40. Taylor relies on Thomas C. Smith, *The Agrarian Origins of Modern*

Japan (Stanford: Stanford University Press, 1959). Smith's analysis is widely accepted by political scientists who use it and make "probabilistic" predictions about Japanese behavior. See, for example, Frank Langdon, *Politics in Japan* (Boston: Little, Brown, 1967). And, of course, scholars in non-Western countries have found that categories derived from Western theories throw light on their own experience, i.e., that their national experience is made more "understandable" by European concepts and categories.

41. For evidence that the "wrenching" effect may not be as great as is often supposed, see Alex Inkeles and David H. Smith, *Becoming Modern: Individual Changes in Six Developing Countries* (Cambridge: Harvard University Press, 1974).

42. In the articles cited earlier.

43. Marvin Surkin, "Sense and Nonsense in Politics," *P.S.*, II (Fall, 1969), 574-575. The quotation does not appear in the version of the article published in the volume Surkin edited with Wolfe. The Left has also been characterized by a tendency to deal with serious intellectual matters with epithets. Thus Daniel Patrick Moynihan does not have to be discussed seriously because he is simply a racist. See Alan Wolfe, "Unthinking About the Thinkable: Reflections on the Failure of the Caucus for a New Political Science," *Politics and Society*, 1 (May, 1971), 393-406.

44. Michael Parenti, "Reviewing the Reviewers: Ideological Bias in the APSR Book Section," *P.S.*, 7 (Fall, 1974), 370-374.

45. Taylor, *loc. cit.*, pp. 54-55, 56.

46. Stanley Rothman, "Marxism and the Paradox of Contemporary Political Thought," *The Review of Politics*, 24 (Spring, 1962), 212-232.

47. John Rawls, *A Theory of Justice* (Cambridge: Belknap Press of Harvard University Press, 1971).

48. William E. Connolly, *The Terms of Political Discourse* (Lexington: D. C. Heath and Company, 1974), pp. 9-44.

49. Gouldner emphasizes this strongly. Not surprisingly he limits his efforts to understanding the social and psychological sources of the views of those he considers to be conservatives.

50. Thus I think that the Left was perfectly correct in criticizing some of those scholars who uncritically lent themselves to rather dubious activities in Vietnam, Chile, and other places around the world.

51. See Edgar Litt and Philip Melanson, "A Peer Group of Liberals: The Profession and Its Public Discontents," paper delivered at the APSA convention, September 1969; Lewis Lipsitz, "The Wolfe Who Cried Caucus: Reform and the Political Science Profession," *Politics and Society*, 1 (August, 1971), 539-541; and, for a survey, E. C. Ladd and S. M. Lipset, "The Politics of American Political Scientists," *P.S.*, 4 (Spring, 1971), 135-144.

52. S. M. Lipset and Gerald M. Schaflander, *Passion and Politics: Student Activism in America* (Boston: Little, Brown, 1971). See also Sidney Hyman, *Youth in Politics: Expectations and Realities* (New York: Basic Books, 1972).

53. Published by Random House.

54. The point is well illustrated by the defensiveness of Easton's 1969 presidential address *vis à vis* the New Left, while at the same time dismissing Straussian critics. Easton, *loc cit.* It is also illustrated by the fact that Parenti's article could receive serious attention in *P.S.*, while "conservative" critiques taking the same position have received short shrift in the past. I have not done my own pseudo count of reviews in the *APSR*, but I'd be willing to bet that a quota-like arrangement for reviews would benefit conservatives far more than radicals.

55. The burden is to constantly re-examine the "liberal" assumptions about reality which undergird a good deal of our research and teaching. Among these assumptions (in Gouldner's terms, background or domain assumptions) I would include the following propositions:

a. While the ideas people hold may influence the manner in which a society functions to a certain extent, the key variables are socio-economic and, among these, class and class interest are central determinants of behavior.

b. Social disorganization in any society is to be blamed on the manner in which the society is organized. Thus in seeking the causes of crime, political discontent or general alienation one should examine the social underpinnings of the society.

   1) Groups calling for change in a more radical direction to correct these abuses are generally humanitarian, even if misguided. The way to deal with them and their constituency is to counsel patience and promote reform.

   2) Groups calling for change in a conservative direction are generally behaving irrationally as the result of status strains or psychological misfunctioning.

c. The purpose of the social order is to promote the opportunity of individuals to maximize their freedom to satisfy their desires at least in non-economics areas. Thus deviant behavior of any kind should be permitted by the society so long as one can not demonstrate that it directly harms other people.

d. Societal problems are inherently solvable by a combination of good will and rational management. If a situation of injustice continues to persist, it must be because self-interested powerful individuals and groups are preventing the development and implementation of reasonable policies.

e. All institutions in the society should be subject to rational scrutiny. Any institutions which can not be defended rationally and which impose restrictions on the individual should be eliminated.

f. People are pretty much alike in terms of their basic needs. Among these needs is full democratic participation, except under those circumstances when a populist regime, in the name of equality, is forced to exercise a certain amount of control in order to modernize.

The above list is not complete; it is certainly something of a caricature, and certainly not all "mainstream" political scientists have held all of these views. Further, I am not persuaded that all of them are false. I am persuaded, however, that they are accepted uncritically by too many scholars.

CHAPTER 2

Education in
Political Commitments

PETER BACHRACH and DOUGLAS BENNETT
Temple University

We plan to argue in this paper that students should learn to formulate commitments in political science classrooms; our case includes both pedagogical and political reasons. We think that learning proceeds better, more seriously, surely more relevantly, in a context where political commitments are formulated and reformulated. Moreover, the ability to form commitments is an important capability in a world in flux, especially within democratic societies where all share in the responsibilities of giving direction. It is our commitments that give a measure of coherence to our various actions, focusing those actions towards our goal; they help in integrating the various aspects of ourselves while allowing us to try to shape a changing world toward one that accords with our hopes and projects. Commitments may be formed well or badly, responsibly or irresponsibly. We plan to argue that learning to form them responsibly, with as full a view of the facts and circumstances as possible, and a sense of the consequences that follow from holding a particular commitment is an essential part of a liberal arts education.

We will proceed in this paper first by making a rather fuller argument in behalf of our contention that the forming of political commitments is an important aspect of learning, and second by trying to show how this learning can best be facilitated by teaching, especially so as to avoid certain obvious dangers such as indoctrination.

I. The Case for Commitment

We are hardly alone in thinking that political science fails to meet its full responsibilities if it insists on confining its view of the proper activities of those in the discipline to scholarly, disinterested research, and to teaching that seeks to create more scholarly, disinterested researchers. In his presidential address to the discipline five years ago, David Easton called for a 'new revolution in political science.'[1] He appealed to the profession to become politicized, to utilize its expertise to rectify the imbalance between the privileged and the masses; but he was wrong in assuming that the simple injection of expert knowledge in the right places would somehow be effective. What the poor, the weak, and the inarticulate desperately require is power, organization, and a sense of identity and purpose, not the rarified advice of political scientists. If our ranks were filled with women and men who possessed the skills and dedication of the late Saul Alinsky, it would be a different matter. But they are not. Even assuming that the expertise of political scientists could be of some benefit to consumer, conservation, and reform groups, Easton's position presupposes that a significant number of the practitioners in the profession have or could easily acquire a taste for practical politics. Undoubtedly a handful aspire to reach the position of a Kissinger or a Bundy, but the overwhelming majority—even the radicals among us —appear to be disposed toward the sedentary life of scholarship and teaching; we are absorbed in studying power, not in wielding it. Ours is the world of theory, of concepts, of methods, of talking rather than doing.

There is an additional and more significant reason why Easton's call for a "new revolution" cannot be taken seriously. His scheme limits the politicalization of the profession to activities of consultation and advising in practical politics, leaving teaching and research in their traditional modes. Although he recognizes that each activity will influence the others, he envisions the post-behavioral revolution coexisting with research that conforms to established scientific methodology.[2] Thus while he urges the profession to respond vigorously to the "crisis" of our time he is hopeful it will also continue to make strides in the expansion of basic knowledge. By underscoring the duality of roles in the profession, he implicitly allows the political scientist two options: to redirect his energies by launching into the struggle to save the nation, or to remain in the role of scientist where the professional payoffs are greater and more secure. It is not surprising, then, that Easton's proposal has had little if any impact in diverting the profession from the tried and routine.

The crisis which alerted Easton more than half a decade ago has not just persisted but deepened considerably; in addition to a continuing deterioration in the legitimacy of governmental authority, the idea of democracy has been stripped of its moral imperatives and come to denote hollowness and hypocrisy. Easton's admonishment to his peers that it is "no longer practical or morally tolerable [for political scientists] to stand on the sidelines when our expertise alerts us to disaster"[3] is consequently more pertinent today than when he wrote. The profession must be prepared to act more boldly than Easton urged, however. In place of his proposal to inject a dose of political responsibility into one phantom arm of the profession, leaving the traditional arms—research and teaching—relatively untouched, we urge such a transformation of all these roles. In this discussion, we will confine our attention to teaching, an activity of some familiarity to all of us.

We contend that to meet both our political responsibilities to the American public and our educational responsibilities to the students in our classes, a chief concern of ours as teachers of political science must be to help students formulate and develop their own political commitments. We must, that is, contribute to equipping students to be fully participant members of a democratic society. For most, this would entail a considerable redirection of focus. We must cease putting emphasis on initiating the novice into the discipline, feeding undergraduate majors such information and technique as to try to reproduce our own kind. Only a tiny fraction of our undergraduates aspire to become professional political scientists, and that is as it should be. For those few, some special provision can be made in the curriculum. The emphasis in the curriculum, however, should be on helping students to become politically aware and capable. We must use the skills, knowledge, and insights we possess as political scientists to assist students in gaining an awareness of their positions in the world, an awareness of the forces that impinge on and shape their lives, and an awareness of the scope of political perspectives, goals, and means open to them.

Neither in our capacity as teachers nor as democrats is it our concern what particular commitments they reach. Rather our commitment is to a process of inquiry focused on helping the student form and *reform* increasingly responsible commitments. This entails a process of inquiry in which students move from a first position—often just an inchoate feeling—to broader and deeper commitments as they acquire the capacity to confront and analyze diverse and often conflicting implications of their commitments, including the consequences for others of their acting or not acting in a certain way.

The teacher can effectively perform his role in this task, we will argue, only if she too shares with students her own political commitments, and her doubts and unresolved problems about them. This entails, of course, her willingness to abandon the usual practice—frequently a failure—of attempting to keep separate and unrevealed her personal convictions from her professional concerns as a political scientist. To persist in a commitment to noncommitment, to inaction over action, is a position vulnerable to the charge of being morally irresponsible and educationally deadening. How can students be expected to treat problems seriously, to be intent upon probing their meanings and ramifications, even at the expense of disrupting values which they cherish, when the teacher is determined to keep separate her personal self and her professional role, when she employs abstract and professional language to disguise all traces of personal voice? To believe that students cannot detect the artificiality of this process is to be naive. If the teacher does not involve herself, her values, her commitments, in the course of discussion, why should they? And if neither side involves self, how deep can the learning experience be?

Education and democracy have been indissolubly linked since the founding of the American republic: there is a tradition here extending from Franklin and Jefferson through John Dewey. Democracy cannot flourish without a well and broadly educated citizenry. And by the same token education proceeds best insofar as students are active participants in the learning process, on a footing that steadily approaches equality. Properly understood, education and democracy have the same goal: the fullest possible development of human capabilities. We could rest our case for urging the formation of political commitments in the classroom on this traditional alliance of democracy and education; but we feel a special urgency in these times that calls for a more pointed argument.

We feel that the American polity is infected with a serious imbalance of power between elites and masses, a power imbalance which is the principal threat to our democracy. Excessive concentration of power corrupts not only the powerful but the powerless as well; the former by breeding in them contempt for ordinary people and a disregard for the democratic process; the latter by weakening the sense of citizenship and the sense of responsibility that flows from it. The growing trend towards nonparticipation in politics among a large sector of the electorate, and the general indifference (until the last moment) toward Watergate reflect the pervasive and corrupting influence of this power imbalance.

Our hope is that the proper sort of education in political science courses can help redress this power imbalance. Students who learn to develop responsible political commitments and a taste for knowledgeable political dialogue in the classroom will carry these outside its confines, voicing their needs and concerns in the public arena. Such students may thus contribute to expanding citizen participation and the reactivation of public debate in civic arenas.

Participation in public affairs is a capability requiring some development; moreover it is the sort of capability that cannot be developed by an individual in isolation. A person needs a group context in which to develop his latent political capacities. This rests on a fundamental premise of democratic theory: as individuals become regular participants in public dialogue they acquire the capacity to relate their own personal troubles to social issues of the times.[4] In the process they form commitments based on real needs, not illusory ones. A major difficulty today is that many people do not have access to the sort of arena in which their latent political capacities can be developed. Our contention is that political science classes (among their other purposes) can function as public arenas for students while they are in college, arenas in which the prevailing climate of civility and reason could provide the conditions most ideally suited to awaken and sharpen the minds of young Americans. As a critical and politically diverse group of students enter the political world, it is likely they will contribute to invigorating public dialogue on fundamental issues confronting the nation—issues, for example, relating to social inequality, corporate power, and democracy. In sharp contrast to the present, the nature and shape of the dialogue would be generated from the bottom up, not top down.

It is important to emphasize here that diversity of views, both in the classroom and in the democratic polity, becomes an essential ingredient to enlightenment, whether the focus is on the evolvement of individual commitments or on national polity. There is good reason, therefore, on both pedagogical and political grounds, why the teacher is neutral to a particular substantive commitment of a student. However, on balance he is likely to invite consideration of the unacceptable at the expense of the accepted position. For at all cost he must help students escape the dogmatic hand of orthodoxy, whether it is currently moored on the Left, Center, or Right.

Our discussion has been largely confined so far to considerations of democracy, but this justification for promoting the formation of commitments in the classroom can be buttressed by considerations from education as well. The guiding intention behind a liberal arts education—in Whitehead's phrase—is to turn "the knowledge of a boy into the power of a man."[5] Its aim is to fit the individual to live a life in wholeness, at the fullest exercise of his given capabilities. Liberal education is liberating education, an education that looks to free for use the capabilities that are locked within any human being.

Liberal education can not be conceived as merely the transmission of knowledge—and we fear that this is what is involved in too much political science teaching. Such an education may produce "the knowledge of a boy" but hardly "the power of a man": knowledge must come to inform the very fiber of a person's being in order for it to free him to live a life of his own. Somehow the ideas that are involved in education must take root in the individual, coming to guide his thought and action. The formation of commitments—we want to argue—is one way that ideas connect themselves to the life of a person. That such commitments are scrutinized through the self-conscious and critical use of reason assures us that this process is fully in keeping with the spirit of a liberal education.

It has been well said that there is no such thing as "education for democracy": education is rather good or bad. But no way of arranging the affairs of human communities has so much need of well-educated women and men as does democracy. In such a society of equals, each must have the capacity to make his own judgments and guide his own conduct. Each must have formed—to the fullest extent possible—a capability for self-direction and self-development. This is particularly important in a world that is changing as rapidly as this one. Almost continuously, new situations must be assessed and new paths must be charted; traditional guides expire daily. If the world is to change into one that accords with our hopes and projects, all of us—as well as the best and the brightest—must take a hand in shaping the future. Our commitments focus our action and understanding to this task.

II. Foundation of Commitment: A Sense of Place

Before we can address ourselves to the manner of teaching that would best facilitate the formation of commitments, we need to establish some conception of the relevant learning process.

To begin, we want to distinguish two different sorts of commitment. The first sort—and this is the sense that comes most readily to mind—is commitment to a course of action or to a manner of conduct. The second sort of commitment is a commitment to a view of the world, to a certain understanding of or perspective on the world.

We want to distinguish between these two sorts of commitment because we will be arguing that they are best addressed at different points in the educational process. They are, of course, related, and in the most intimate ways. *How* they are related will have bearing on the order in which these two sorts of commitment are developed in the learning process. From a purely logical point of view we might suppose that a commitment to a view of the world is prior to a commitment to a course of action: a particular perspective of politics would present certain courses of political action as much more appropriate than others, and thus lead us towards adopting them.

We are inclined to think, however, that the psychology of human learning places a commitment to a course of action prior to a commitment to a view of the world. Certain courses of action lead us into having certain kinds of experiences which tend toward our forming a particular perspective on politics.

Underlying the formation of both sorts of commitment is a kind of learning we feel is vital to any sort of effective classroom education. We call this lesson "a sense of self"; what is involved is the development in the student of a conception of his own place in the world, of his relationship to the issues under consideration in the course. Only if the student sees herself as directly involved in the matters under consideration will she risk enough of herself to permit any commitments to be brought into question. And of course that same sense of self-involvement assists any classroom learning by heightening student interest in the material. If students do not find themselves located in the issues under consideration, they may go through the motions of considering them, but their analysis will be artificial, void of meaning. It will not challenge their values; it will not cause intellectual anguish or even a ripple of disturbance. They will probably forget the matter as they step out of class.

The first task in teaching, then, is to bring to consciousness what the students already believe by virtue of their personal experience about themselves and society. Before any background is presented, before any assigned materials are considered, the students must be asked to locate themselves firmly in the issues. If an extended consideration of the nature of justice is planned, the teacher may want to begin by asking the students their opinions on some current issue involving justice (for example the pardoning of Richard Nixon, or the question of amnesty for war deserters). These opinions can then be shown to involve the seeds of various conceptions of justice that will be discussed and developed later; but students will already have provisionally identified themselves with one of these conceptions.[6]

A colleague of ours who was teaching a class containing a substantial number of policemen complained that the class was bored and somewhat put off by a series of introductory lectures he gave over the first few weeks trying to portray the basic shape of an urban community. They learned little or nothing from those lectures. And why? Because policemen seemed to have no place in his portrayal of the community. They couldn't see themselves in it. At the beginning of the course our colleague had not known that so many policemen would be enrolled. Had he known that (he said) he would have accorded policemen a more prominent place in the lectures. We always face that problem, however, not knowing who the students are at the beginning, not knowing what preconceptions and beliefs they have. To a certain extent, they do not know who they are either, probably never having been placed in a context where they had to face these preconceptions and beliefs. Part of the growth that should be occurring in education is the development of a measure of self-understanding. Rather than trying to perform the task of location *for* our students (as our colleague would have done) we think it better to ask students to locate themselves in the issues. With the class of policemen, the teacher could have begun by asking them to picture the communities they have worked in, what the people there did and why, how they themselves acted as policemen there and why. These portraits might never have been given explicit rendering before, but once formulated the teacher could present his materials providing a different picture, perhaps challenging key elements in the policemen's picturings. Once located—self-placed—in the world under consideration, the policemen could not easily stand to one side, aloofly.

Developing a sense of self is crucial for beginning the consideration of an issue or subject, but it can also be helpful for initiating discussion of materials in any class meeting. The particular subject matter is relatively unimportant; what counts is what is done with it. Almost any reading assigned to a class can seem alien to the students if the teacher does not make a conscientious effort to help them "connect" to it. Whether it be Plato's *Republic*, or Banfield's *The Unheavenly City* we can say—at some risk of being misunderstood—that the primary focus must not be on the question "what did he say?" but rather "what does it mean to you? Where does it find you?"

Developing a sense of self is the recommended beginning point for consideration, but we hardly mean to confine the subject matter to the immediate interests and horizons of the students. That would fail to allow for growth, and would strip the inquiry of intellectual challenge. The "stand" that a student takes in locating himself in the material amounts to the embryo of a commitment, but to rest content with such a commitment might involve accepting an irresponsible, ill-considered notion.

III. Commitment to a Course of Action

From the starting point of a sense of place or a sense of self-location we will be wanting to help our students develop mature and responsible commitments through the consideration and reconsideration of tentative positions and of various alternatives to these.

First on our agenda is the commitment to a course of action or a manner of conduct. The general strategy to be employed here by the teacher is to help students trace the implications of their initial stands, trying to broaden and deepen such an initial stand until it covers a full range of contingency for human action. Such an initial stand may—at the beginning—amount to nothing more than a gut feeling about what is to be done in a particular situation. In taking such a stand, the student may fail to offer any reasons justifying this gut feeling. In working toward the development of a responsible commitment, the primary tasks of the teacher will be to push the students to formulate the reasons or principles underlying their stands, and then to encourage them to apply these newly formulated principles to analogous situations. Several outcomes are possible from this sequence. The student may find that the principles do direct him towards what seems to be an appropriate course of action in the analogous situation. Or they may direct him towards an unacceptable course of action, in which case he has a number of choices (which the teacher will want to make sure the student keeps before himself). He can try to show how the second situation is not really analogous, thus limiting the application of the principles; he can try to refashion the principles so that they lead to appropriate action in both cases; or he can abandon his initial stand altogether, recognizing that it rests on an objectionable sort of commitment. This sequence of taking a stand, formulating an underlying principle, and then trying to extend that principle to like situations can be repeated a number of times.

Differing and conflicting stands on an issue by members of the class can not only stimulate thought and heighten the sense of importance of the issue, but can also, providing the discussion is skillfully handled, lead students to a reexamination of their positions on a deeper and more sophisticated level of understanding. Materials that are read outside class can present other positions which students may want to try to adopt as their own, or which they may want to react against. The application of certain principles to a situation may well turn on certain factual considerations which can be introduced through readings. The object throughout this process is not only to encourage students to develop, sharpen, and/or reevaluate their positions, but equally important to acquire the taste and capacity to look beyond their direct interests and narrow horizons towards a fuller view of the world and of their place in it as a member of society and humanity. Stated somewhat differently, the ultimate objective is to help students to develop a toughness of mind and a sensitivity that lead them to see problems in their commitments and thus to question and reformulate those commitments through the course of their lives.

Conducting a class so as to encourage students to formulate commitments and scrutinize them critically calls for a rather different manner of teaching than is normally encountered. The teacher must devolve upon the students a fair measure of responsibility for the direction and shape of classroom discussions. Instead of entering with a fixed agenda of material to be covered or of questions to be asked, the teacher should encourage the students to establish the starting point for discussion in taking an initial stand—that is, through forming a sense of self. What transpires in the classroom will involve working within the avenues of development opened up by the students' initial positions rather than within some framework established solely by the teacher. What is wanted from the teacher is an ability to respond to the student's ideas and formulations in ways that provide depth and continuity to the discussion. Often this requires the reformulation of a student's point to reveal implications or difficulties she may not have seen. For any student contribution, this sequence can be recommended: the viewpoint should be accepted and acknowledged as a helpful contribution; if the idea is unclear to other class members, the student should be encouraged to elaborate it; and finally (and only after these first two steps) the point can be reformulated by the teacher to show possible avenues for further development, or a new context can be proposed by the teacher within which to consider the viewpoint.

The stands and commitments that are explored here must be legitimately and recognizably the students'. Otherwise they may feel they are being manipulated into being mere mouthpieces for the teacher to play on. Once a position is proposed by a student, she must be made to feel some worth in her contribution, and the other students must be invited within its boundaries, encouraged to see its plausibility and merits. Once the class has been gathered within the position, they are well situated to explore its ramifications with some possibility of coming to acknowledge it as the basis of their commitment to a course of action. If the students explore a number of such positions in this manner, the commitment they adopt stands a fair chance of having been responsibly and rationally chosen.

IV. Commitment to a View of the World

We have yet to consider the second sort of commitment, the commitment to a view of the world. How we look at the world affects what we see. Our interest in the subject matter shapes the questions we are wanting answered. The concepts we employ in framing questions and answers act as lenses that permit us to see some matters with particular sharpness while casting others into dimness or obscurity. If different perspectives open different windows on the world, then clearly there is a choice to be made here.

We need not, and ought not, draw from this, however, that the best policy is one of simple promiscuity among points of view, moving among approaches with only the intention of trying several. Some perspectives open onto barren vistas and others (at least at certain times and for certain purposes) prove particularly revealing. If we come to settle on a particular approach or point of view—and most serious intellects do—then we can take that choice of perspective to be in the manner of a commitment. It is this choice of a perspective, of a set of conceptual lenses, that we have in mind in speaking of a commitment to a point of view.

How are we to teach here, where such commitments are concerned? There can be no ducking this question if commitments are inextricably involved in the way we look at the world. Teaching with regard to these commitments is harder than teaching with regard to commitments to courses of action.

We should note, at the outset, how different are the standard practices of political science teachers with regard to these two kinds of commitments. With the first kind—to a course of action—most political science teachers tend to try to avoid the subject altogether, even to the point of concealing the fact of their own commitments and positions. Their justification is that they are trying to avoid indoctrinating the students into blindly accepting their positions. It is interesting to note that most political scientists make neither an attempt to hide their particular commitment to one paradigm, nor help their students make an informed and responsible choice. That they may be indoctrinating their students into a blind acceptance of their own view of the world seems not to concern them at all.

A student came to see one of us about a proposed project that he wanted to embark on, and the notion of ideology came up on several occasions. On each mention, without fail, the student repeated or alluded to a three-part conception of ideology he had evidently learned in some class: "there are three parts to an ideology: world view, strategy, and tactics"; it came out like a litany. If this is all there is to it, the example might be trivial; but just as likely this catechism is a part of some more fully articulated conception of ideology. That conception may help him to understand some things about ideologies, but he surely has no notion at all that there are other conceptualizations involving the notion of ideology which would allow him to see the world in other ways. That he has formed a commitment here (or that one has been formed for him) he has no notion at all. His vision has been locked in place by an all-too successful bit of teaching. If all the materials that a teacher presents to the class proceed out of one perspective or approach, there is always that danger that a student will accept the viewpoint in an uncritical fashion. Suppose, then, that the teacher presents more than one approach? The risk of indoctrination is reduced, but now, however, there is substantial risk of confusion. If the students are not aware that two approaches are at hand they may try to accept both simultaneously. Even if this is avoided, there is still likely to be no real progress toward the student forming his own commitments. As long as the teacher is *presenting*, the student is relegated to choosing among pre-formed and pre-digested alternatives. If we risk indoctrinating our students, in insisting that ours are the only acceptable answers, we just as surely indoctrinate them in insisting that ours are the only appropriate questions. One goal of teaching—a goal that works towards students forming their own intellectual commitments to help them be autonomous, fully participating members of a democratic community—is to bring our students to formulate their own questions and to fashion their own conceptual tools.

In general what is wanted is to have students propose a way of looking at the world whose potential and limitations can then be explored by the class. Getting students to propose a conceptual framework, however, could be quite a chore. Happily, we have an alternative that has been prepared by the consideration of a commitment to a course of action. Such a commitment to a course of action must presuppose some perspective within which sequences of events and chains of occurrence are framed. In anticipating courses of action we must have some picture of the world within which action is envisioned. Rather than asking students to propose a perspective *de novo*, then, we can help them recognize and assess the implicit views of the world they have already composed in forming commitments to courses of action.

Teaching toward this sort of commitment should proceed in much the same manner as teaching toward commitment to a course of action: the teacher encouraging the student to formulate an initial position, inviting other students to see the plausibility of the perspective, then helping the students to see implications and problems. An example may be of assistance. Suppose we have a student who has formed a commitment to furthering women's liberation. Suppose further that this commitment to a course of action has gone through some careful scrutiny in the classroom. What is wanted now is to bring her to see that this commitment rests on another commitment, a commitment to a certain way of looking at the world. The teacher gradually draws out the important conceptualizations that are involved here: for example the notion that liberation is directly linked to the idea of equality of opportunity for a particular *group* of people. The implications of this view must be traced. It might come to trouble such a student that to the degree to which equality of opportunity for women fosters equality between the sexes, it promotes inequality among individuals; for by expanding opportunity for a greater number of people to compete for a relatively fixed number of choice positions, it creates a significantly greater number of losers rather than winners. Once this point is adequately analyzed and perhaps challenged, the discussion may focus on a number of issues, such as the relationship between individual freedom and meritocracy, the impact of women's liberation on socio-economic institutions and life-styles, and perhaps on the meaning of human liberation. A discussion of this kind may lead the student to reformulate her notion of women's liberation, a reformulation that would take into consideration normative and socio-economic issues hitherto ignored. It may amount, in other words, to her viewing her commitment to a course of action from a broader and deeper perspective on the world.

V. The Hidden Curriculum

We have been considering the formation of commitments in a very special kind of environment, the classroom. For some purposes, this is the very best kind of environment: it encourages quiet-tempered reflection, and the thorough consideration of alternatives. There is one possibility, however, of the classroom's being a less than an ideal environment for the formation of commitments; the students may not take seriously what goes on, they may not see it as having a bearing on what goes on outside the classroom. In such a case students may not "carry over" the commitments they form inside the classroom to apply to their lives outside. Somehow, students must be brought to believe that commitments and understandings formed at school don't just apply to school, to the getting of good grades and the earning of degrees. If they see the classroom as just a sophisticated game with rules that are peculiar to it and that don't apply in the "real world," then these commitments formed in the classroom will not inform their conduct once they leave it.

In large measure, whether students take classroom learning as having a serious bearing on their lives depends on expectations and orientations they bring with them to college. But insofar as these expectations can be altered by the teacher it will happen through the manner of teaching, especially the way the teacher presents himself, rather than through the course content.

In addition to a manifest curriculum of subjects and materials offered for learning, teachers have a "hidden curriculum" of lessons conveyed. Through the practice of grading students, for example, students learn to be competitive with one another. Another example: they learn to be individualistic through being asked to work on projects, papers, and tests alone, by themselves, rather than with others, in groups.

It is also through this hidden curriculum that students learn how seriously to take the commitments formed in the classroom, whether to view them as touching their lives outside school.

As a student, one of us had an introductory course in philosophy in which the subject matter touched on a number of key religious beliefs including the existence of God. In class discussions almost the entire class professed atheism. "How many of you go to church?" the teacher asked on a number of occasions; "and why" when it became evident that some of us did. "Will you go to church when you're married?" "Will you send your children to Sunday school?" He made it clear to us that we needed to take seriously the commitments we professed in his classroom. He insisted that our intellectual commitments square with our everyday conduct. It would be a mistake, though, to conclude that he succeeded in making us take seriously our own classroom commitments simply because he raised the issue for consideration. He succeeded more because he presented himself as a person who took his own view of the world seriously, and because he treated us with respect, as if what we said was meant to be taken seriously.

One aspect of the hidden curriculum here comes with the model that the teacher presents to the class. If he evidences himself as a person with commitments whose actions outside are congruent with professions inside the classroom, his students may find that influential in molding their own characters.

The more common practice among political science teachers is to analyze courses of action in order to reveal their probable consequences. No attempt is made, however, to push toward a rational decision. The analysis stops just short of that. If any conclusion is reached, it is likely to be that "all the facts are not yet in," so commitment to a course of action must be postponed. Students may draw either of two lessons from this. They may take on a commitment to non-commitment if they carry over what they learn in class to their lives outside school. In following the example the teacher presents in class in forgoing commitments, they may become chary of ever placing them behind a course of action. Alternately, the students may discern that the teacher is separating his professional understanding of politics from his commitments. Students are able to distinguish a serious intellectual undertaking from a sophisticated game played to provoke them. They may play at the game, for grades or for amusement, but they are unlikely to form any commitments that will be carried out of the classroom.

If the teacher does show himself in the classroom as a person who is not hesitant to form and stand by commitments, he can act as a model for the manner in which such commitments are formed. He does them no service if he makes that seem easy. The best way to encourage students to engage in the rather painful activity of probing the soundness of their own thinking is for the teacher to engage openly in a process of questioning and self-doubt. (One unfortunate lesson of the hidden curriculum conveyed by too many teachers is that the matters under consideration are "easy for me"—the teacher—but "hard for you"—the students. That lesson is conveyed merely by teachers' failing to let the student witness the effort involved, seeing only the end result of that process, smoothly presented.)

The hidden curriculum is involved in a second way. The teacher not only presents herself as a model to the students; she also helps them form an image of themselves in the way she treats them. If she takes their ideas seriously, they are more likely to take those ideas seriously as well, both in and out of the classroom. Nothing conveys that so well as the teacher's showing herself to have something to learn from the students. If she listens closely to their ideas, reformulating her conceptions in light of their contributions, they will gain self-esteem for their own capabilities. One of us was an outside evaluator of the teaching quality of an instructor in a small liberal arts college. A written evaluation from one student (these were part of the record) read: "I work for [him] because I respect him; I have a moral obligation to do well. His courses are not "academic"; ideas and issues emerge as important to my concerns. He compels me to make the link between my own experiences and what goes on in class. He questions value judgments behind one's position, not because he wants the 'right answer,' but because he wants to know." This is very much the sort of teaching we have in mind, but the last point is the one we want to feature here: the teacher showing himself to care personally about what the student thinks.

VI. Education and Indoctrination: Concluding Remarks

The learning sequence we have been trying to sketch seeks to make students active rather than passive learners. Students are encouraged to begin by finding themselves in the problems and materials under consideration. They are asked to view the world that is under consideration as their world, the world that they live in and will continue to live in. Having established such a sense of self, the teacher strives to bring to the surface the gut-feelings and inclinations that the students bring with them into the classroom. These can be seen as the embryos of commitments, but the goal of the teacher is surely not to assist students in settling into these initial positions. Instead, she wants to encourage them to use these inclinations and gut-feelings to explore the subject matter. The questions for which answers are to be sought will be their questions, questions that genuinely puzzle and trouble them, not questions that the teacher has proposed for them to answer. If our students are to become lifelong seekers after the truth, they must begin posing their own questions while they are still in school.

As the class pursues questions of their own asking, the teacher's major task and responsibility becomes one of insuring that questions are pursued thoroughly, with clarity and rigor. Students must be pushed to encounter new facts and new contexts, many of them uncongenial. Through readings and other presentations of material, the teacher can set before the students such unfamiliar facts and contexts. Moreover, the teacher should see that the students are faced with viewpoints and commitments that are divergent from their own. Students should be encouraged to see the plausibility of perspectives that are at odds with their own as well as to mount arguments against them, in defense of their own perspective. Finally, the students must be pushed and coaxed to follow these nascent commitments to their full and final consequences, even if these are unexpected and troubling.

Throughout this process, many initial positions will be expanded and deepened. Equally likely, however, as students attend to new facts and troubling consequences, many initial positions will be abandoned or seriously revised. New positions need to be put to the same kind of scrutiny, of course.

This view of the place of commitments in political science education places the emphasis on the process of forming and reforming commitments rather than on the adoption of any 'final' commitment. Students must come to know when to abandon an unwise or unwarranted position as well as how to defend a well-founded one and to use it to illuminate the world both in and out of the classroom.

By way of concluding, we might try to lay to rest the most serious worry that could be entertained about this kind of teaching that seeks to help form political commitments: how can we be assured that there is no danger of indoctrinating students into adopting our own commitments? This danger is one that is present in any kind of teaching. We feel it is best avoided by political scientists who have an overriding commitment to provide conditions intended to stimulate student thinking rather than simply to impart information and ideas that it is believed students ought to know.

Teachers who recognize the above are likely also to see that the mere dissemination of truth is not likely to stimulate students to think, that it may instead smother their intellectual interest and strengthen their propensity to accept uncritically the pronouncements of authority figures. What teachers principally become aware of, in other words, is not the danger of indoctrination but rather the futility of telling students what is true. In John Dewey's words, they recognize that:

> No thought, no idea, can possibly be conveyed as an idea from one person to another. When it is told, it is, to the one to whom it is told, another given fact, not an idea. The communication may stimulate the other person to realize the question for himself and to think out a like idea, or it may smother

his intellectual interest and suppress his dawning effort at thought. But what he *directly* gets cannot be an idea. Only by wrestling with the conditions of the problem at first hand, seeking and finding his own way out, does he think.[7]

Applying Dewey's insight to the political science class, when students are absorbed in dialogue, when they "wrestle" with the problem "at first hand" (within a context of their own choice), any expression of belief by the teacher can be more readily translated from a fact to an idea by students and critically appraised by them in light of contrasting and conflicting ideas that have been generated in the course of the discussion. In the interest of enriching the dialogue and pitting authority against authority, it is helpful if works are assigned which confront one another, especially the teacher's position.

In considering the problem of indoctrination, a distinction must be made, on the one hand, between helping a student discover who she is and what political ideas and goals she believes worth supporting, and on the other an attempt to persuade her of the truth of a particular doctrine or ideology, democratic or otherwise. In adhering to the first and not the second route, the profession's commitment would be focused upon strengthening the fundamental requisite of a democratic polity, namely, the existence of a significantly large proportion of citizens who have acquired the capacity to care about things political and the ability to appraise political issues in light of well-considered positions. In a world that is changing as rapidly as this one, free women and men must possess the capacity to grasp those changes, to adjust to them where necessary, and to direct them where possible and appropriate. In the university these capabilities can effectively be nurtured and developed in political science classes that are relatively free of indoctrination. And such classes are those in which students, through being participants in meaningful discussions that range from heated to profound debate gain a sense of the importance of politics and a reasonably intelligent way of thinking politically. They are classes in which the teacher, through his involvement in being teacher and learner at the same time, has no hesitancy in expressing his deep concerns, his doubts, and his commitments. He does so knowing that his ultimate commitment as a teacher and as a democrat is to the development of his students as thinking and politically caring human beings.

FOOTNOTES

1. David Easton, "The New Revolution in Political Science," *American Political Science Review*, LXIII (December, 1969), 1051-1062.

2. Thus instead of proposing a single professional organization to serve both purposes, he suggests establishing a second organization that would focus exclusively on current social issues. *Ibid.*, p. 1060.

3. *Ibid.*

4. See C. Wright Mills, *The Sociological Imagination* (New York: Oxford University Press, 1959).

5. A. N. Whitehead, *The Aims of Education and Other Essays* (New York: Free Press, 1929, 1967), p. 27.

6. For a useful discussion of techniques for helping students locate themselves in issues, see Sidney Simon, Leland Howe, and Howard Kirschenbaum, *Values Clarification: A Handbook of Practical Strategies for Teachers and Students* (New York: Hart Publishing Co., 1972).

7. John Dewey, *Democracy and Education* (New York: Free Press, 1966), pp. 159-160.

CHAPTER 3

The Politicization of Everything:
On the Limits of Politics in Political Education

HEINZ EULAU
Stanford University

There is a room with a view—a "studio" it is called—looking out, in a southerly direction, over the elegant, formal gardens of the Villa Serbelloni and the red-tiled roofs of the ancient town of Bellagio, at the foot of the promontory between lakes Como and Lecco. Across the lakes, through the late-summer haze, loom the granite mountains that ultimately reach the Po Valley; and beyond there lie the Italian peninsula and the *forum Romanum*. Today's forum is a quiet, solitary, and awry patch of ruins, but it is the place where Cicero once delivered his political orations and where Caesar was assassinated by his political enemies. There is no chance of mistaking the studio as a *concept* with the forum as a *concept;* of confusing the privacy, tranquility and integrity of the studio with the sociality, tumultuousness, and turpitude of the forum; of identifying knowledge of political things with political action.

What can one possibly say, from this vantage point and by way of novel statement, about education, political education, education in political science, or the politicization of education, that has not been said before and better? Alas, it is the perspective of the "room with a view" that challenges the Proposition—as I shall refer to it for brevity's sake throughout the paper—that "the teaching of political science is itself a political act." My gut reaction is that the Proposition is logically absurd, theoretically trivial, empirically false, ethically undesirable, morally wrong, and politically dangerous. However, gut reaction is not enough. There has to be rational argument if a case against acceptance of the Proposition is to be made. But is rational argument possible if denial of the Proposition is itself considered a political act—if there is a politicization of everything, and if no limits

are set to the politicization of political science as an educational enterprise?

These limits are disinterested and dispassionate scholarship. The
teacher may not always be able to stay within these limits, for he is,
though not a political, certainly a public, actor; the scholar has no
choice but to maintain the limits in order to remain a scholar. Max
Weber, eminently sensitive to the problem, once observed that "every
young man who feels called to scholarship has to realize clearly that
the task before him has a double aspect. He must qualify not only as
scholar but also as a teacher. And the two do not at all coincide. One
can be a preeminent scholar and at the same time an abominably poor
teacher."

Weber did not specify the characteristics of an abominably poor
teacher, but he would have undoubtedly included politically partial
or one-sided presentation of subject-matter. One need only turn
Weber's observation around and ask, "Is it possible to be a good
teacher and at the same time an abominably poor scholar?" to find
the appropriate answer. Because good scholarship is indispensable to
good teaching, the criteria and values of scholarship must guide the
teacher as he leaves the privacy of his study and enters the classroom.
It is impossible to conceive of a teacher who lives by the Proposition
and is also a good scholar. That, on logico-empirical, ethical and
moral grounds, the Proposition and the vocation of teacher-scholar
do not mix is the burden of my argument.

The Logico-Empirical Argument—Of True and False

To be theoretically valid and empirically acceptable, the Proposition must be falsifiable by evidence to the contrary. Falsifiability in
turn requires that there be a logical rival hypothesis, to the effect that
political science teaching is *not* itself a political act. Only if the null
hypothesis can be entertained does the Proposition have logical status
as a theoretically valid and empirically viable hypothesis. If the rival
or null hypothesis cannot be rejected, the Proposition may well be
considered disconfirmed, though it does not represent a fool-proof
test for the truth of the rival hypothesis. The latter can be countered
by a further rival hypothesis, and so on. On the other hand, if the
rival hypothesis can be rejected, this is not sure proof for the Proposition but merely would strengthen one's belief in its validity.

All of this is rather elementary, but the logical requirement that would validate the theoretical status of the Proposition involves more than simply transforming it into the null hypothesis. It requires an assumption often ignored in the routine empirical testing of the null hypothesis. If the premise underlying the Proposition as the original or substantive hypothesis is of a kind that permits only confirmation of the hypothesis and only rejection of the rival hypothesis, the logic of proof cannot be anything but fallacious.

The logical problem, then, turns on the premise implicit in the Proposition. What is the premise? And is it such that the rival hypothesis, if not confirmed on being tested, can at least not be rejected? The premise seems to be that there is no condition antecedent to the teaching of political science that is not political, and that there is no condition consequent to the teaching of political science that is not political. If both the cause and the effect of teaching political science are political, then the teaching of political science must be a political act. The premise underlying the Proposition is "the politicization of everything."

It is clear that the premise on which the Proposition is based precludes giving the rival hypothesis a fair test. If the antecedents and consequences of teaching political science are all political, there is no way to show that the rival proposition cannot be rejected. The premise of the policitization of everything denies, out of hand so to speak, the negation of the Proposition. For the negation of the Proposition, it follows from the premise, is itself a political act. There is only one possible inference from the premise that everything is political: the Proposition is always true and its denial is always false.

The premise of the politicization of everything does not permit falsification of the Proposition. But a hypothesis that is always true and whose negation is always false is trivial, and a logic of derivation which simultaneously affirms the antecedent and the consequent is fallacious.

Yet so contagious is the current vogue of the ancient art of political sophistry that serious people take its assertions seriously. The absurdity of the logic involved threatens to become common coin. It is an impenetrable logic: by not conceding in its premise any limits to the political in human thought and action, the logic is one of "infinite regression." It does not matter whether one affirms or denies that teaching political science is itself a political act; and it does not matter whether one states the problem in terms of hypothesis or null hypothesis. Given the premise that all events (and non-events) are political in nature, both types of formulation are necessarily political acts, and so on *ad infinitum*.

Rather than being profound in the sense of opening up new insights or understandings, the premise underlying the Proposition trivializes politics. If everything is political, nothing is political. The premise does not supply a single independent criterion for discriminating between the truth or falsity of an assertion about education in political science, for there is no discrimination between the political and the non-political.

A system of thought that postulates politics as something immanent and universal in all human action and in all human events is fully closed. Closure means that no relevant variables have been omitted and error is not possible. The omnipresence of politics cannot be denied, for no case disproving it is conceivable. Although pretending to be "theoretical," the conception of politics as something immanent and universal in all human action is only a monstrous tautology predicated on a metapolitical belief. Rather than saying anything about the real world of politics or education in politics, the Proposition is devoid of substance.

Further pursuit of the Proposition would seem to be rather futile, were it not for its potentially dangerous impact on rational discourse concerning the relationship between politics and scholarship or education in political science. If one *suspects* the denial of the Proposition to be itself a political act, as the logic of infinite regression requires, there is introduced into discourse a mode of thought that hypostatizes suspicion into a legitimate principle of rationality. This mode of thought has a catching effect even on those who would want to escape it: one is tempted to suspect those advancing the Proposition of having ulterior motives—of not saying what they really mean. What, one wonders, makes a person promote a proposition that requires a trivial premise and an absurd logic? But at this point one enters the psycho-logic and leaves the logic of discourse about politics and education. To avoid being drawn into the bottomless pit of political psychologizing, it is of the ultmost importance to contest the Proposition not on psychological but on logical, empirical, ethical and moral grounds.

An empirically viable approach to the problem of the relationship between politics and education about politics proceeds from the assumption that political action, on the one hand, and education about politics, on the other hand, are analytically distinct aspects of human behavior. Although their discourse was largely normative, political philosophers from Plato to John Stuart Mill have assumed the analytic distinction between political action and political education, for only this assumption allows one to speculate about the *proper* relationship between them. It is the distinction between political education and action (unlike the isomorphism implicit in the Proposition) that makes the problem of exploring the relationship interesting and non-trivial. Empirical inquiry based on the premise of a distinction between political action and education will come to different conclusions as to what the relationship is in one or another political context, and it does therefore not prejudge the findings.

Education is always an intervening process—the process of bringing knowledge to bear on subsequent behavior. Education assumes that there is something worthy to be known that through teaching and learning can be transmitted for later use. An education in political science must make the same assumption. Its task is to transmit political knowledge so that this knowledge may be made—though it need not be made—germane to political practice. But political education is not itself political action; for if it were political action, it could not perform its task of transmitting political knowledge. Whether it performs its task well is a matter of empirical study that requires both a definition of what "good" political science education is (on which there is disagreement) and relevant evidence.

Political science education is a form of political education but not the only form. A political education may be had from sources other than theoretical or empirical knowledge—from "experience" directly gained through political participation or from "empathy" with the political experiences of others as conveyed in novels or biographies or plays. But political experience through participation makes for know-how rather than knowledge, and political empathy makes for sensitivity rather than knowledge. Political experience and empathy are "educational" only insofar as they become sources of reflection or understanding, in the sense that they are generalized to political circumstances other than those from which they derive and are possibly transmitted to others who may apply what has been learned from experience or empathy.

Whether rooted in knowledge, experience or empathy, political education is different from political action; it follows past action and precedes future action but is never itself political action. If political education were not distinct from political action, nothing would stand in the way of reversing the Proposition and asserting that "a political act is itself an education in political science," or perhaps "political action is itself political education." These statements are obviously fallacious. For they imply that whatever the political act or the political action, it *is* education. There is no room in this "education-through-action" or "action-as-education" for discrimination as to just what education and action are all about.

The Ethical Argument—Of Good and Bad

Even if, for the sake of argument, the Proposition were logically and empirically viable, this would not eliminate the bothersome ethical question of whether teaching political science *should be* a political act. As an ethical command the Proposition can only mean that political values should take precedence in political science education over the values normally associated with the creation and transmission of knowledge. What will happen, one may ask, if political values take precedence over educational values? Let us consider two scenarios—one of the politically totally open, and one of the politically totally closed, society.

The politically totally closed society, enforcing only one value or system of values, is the simple case, for here the criteria associated with scholarly discovery and communication are altogether precluded from entering the educational curriculum or, should they enter, subject to persecution and elimination. In this educational situation there is no concern with the validity or reliability of assertions, the move from evidence to inference, the objectivity and truth of knowledge. Respect for scholarly values has not even a fighting chance in the monistic educational system of the closed society.

By way of contrast, in the politicized pluralistic system, the teacher of political science is free to promote any political value he prefers. As there are many teachers with diverse political views and values, the educational situation would seem to constitute that competitive marketplace of ideas where truth is thought to emerge even if the ideas themselves are partial, biased, odious or false. However, whether this represents an educationally optimal situation is a matter of argument and cannot be simply taken for granted. The requirements of sound education in political science are not satisfied by the raw intellectual fares offered in the marketplace of political conflict. If anything, in this situation the criteria of disinterested and dispassionate scholarship are even more needed than they are under mercifully less politicized academic conditions.

These are, of course, "ideal type" constructs and not empirically viable educational systems. Yet, there are real-world situations which come uncomfortably close to these ideal types. One knows of the excesses of a politicalized education in fascist and communist regimes. Paradoxically, these excesses may also occur in politicized pluralistic systems where they are justified by the doctrine that education is a political act. The harassment of teachers whose presentation of unpopular views or opposition to preferred ideas is considered obnoxious is a matter of record. It is irrelevant whether the presentation is balanced or the criticism supported by evidence, for the criteria of judgment in these situations are not the criteria associated with science and scholarship but political criteria. Under the Proposition it is not necessary to demonstrate that the teacher has violated the criteria of objective scholarship and responsible education; it is sufficient for teaching to be perceived as a political act in order to deny the values of scholarly inquiry as being appropriate to education and to unleash the forces of academic know-nothingness. The gladiators of the ideological Right and Left are always ready to do battle.

As a normative assertion, as a statement of what ought to be, the Proposition is clearly destructive of the criteria and values commonly connected with science, scholarship, and education. All of this is not to deny that political views and values enter the scholarly or scientific study of politics at many points, from the conception of an investigation to its conclusion and interpretation. And, as a result, they necessarily enter the teaching of political science. This intrusion is not *ipso facto* destructive of due process of inquiry and education. There are political values especially conducive to the flowering of science and scholarship, such as the classical liberalism of the humanist tradition. But insofar as political values or preferences obstruct or disturb the scholarly process and product, they are "biases" that can and should be treated as "errors." They can be identified, isolated and "controlled for" in very much the same way as one controls for other errors in the scholarly enterprise—errors of conceptualization, errors of observation, sampling or measurement errors, or errors in logical inference. In other words, bias stemming from value commitment or preferences can and should be neutralized.

Let me be explicit if short:[1] the *neutralization* of values or preferences as biases that are treated as errors should not be confused with value *neutrality*, the assumption that science is or can be totally value-free, or with *neutralism* as philosophical indifference to values. On the contrary, it is a high degree of sensitivity to values and an awareness of the biases they can introduce into the scholarly enterprise that lie at the base of the argument. One need not for a moment believe that value bias can be fully eliminated from the study of political affairs and from education in political science; but the study of politics and education in political science can also not be allowed to degenerate into a morass of prejudice and subjectivity. It is for this reason that the values of scholarship must take precedence over the values of politics in the teaching of political science. The teaching of political values should be an important component of the curriculum in political science. Because political behavior and action are purposive and goal-oriented, the ethical nature of the means and ends of politics, and the ethical issues arising out of the relationship between them, should be high on the agenda of political science teaching. For only knowledge of different values and value systems can make for the studious discrimination among values that is required to prevent values or preferences from biasing the knowledge of political things.

The decline of political ethics as a disciplinary concern has been due not just to the rise of scientific positivism and the growing multiverse of ideologies, but also to the failure of ethical teaching about politics to be a dispassionate and disinterested enterprise. Sheldon Wolin has argued that "most of the important theories were a response to crisis; they have reflected a conviction either that political action might destroy certain civilized values and practices, or that it might be the means for deliverance from evils, such as injustice or oppression."[2] And this explains for him "why most political theories contain radical critiques."[3] The vocation of the political theorist is not only to interpret but also to change the world. But this activist interpretation of the theorist's role is as ill-conceived as the charge of complacency Wolin makes against "official" political science.[4] If "complacency" means being disinterested and dispassionate, Wolin's characterization of political science seems to be its best defense.

Dissatisfaction with political philosophy is likely to be forthcoming if those who teach it do so without being truly philosophical about it. "Being ethical" has many meanings, but the equation of teaching political science with being a form of political action does not strike me as worthy of being called an ethical position. An important criterion for judging the vocation of political theory is that the teacher of political theory be sensitive to the same biases that also afflict the teacher of a scientific politics. Indeed, I would think that one should expect this even more from the political "theorists" than from the political "scientists." Being critical of the biases of others but cultivating one's own, as do those for whom the teaching of political science is itself a political act, is a perversion of scholarship and education.

Of course, the teacher of political science and the teacher of political ethics should be free to express their own political values and convictions. Such expression is a prerequisite for disinterested and dispassionate teaching, for only what is expressed can be subjected to scholarly scrutiny. But self-scrutiny—maintaining doubt as to one's belief and admitting the possibility of error—must accompany the scrutiny of others if teaching political science or ethics is to be something other than a political act.

There is an ironic element in the position of those who see the vocation of the political scientist not only as one of radical critique but also of political action—of changing the world. They inveigh against dispassion and disinterestedness in teaching about politics because, they allege, it reduces political science education to "mere technique," the "training" of the young in the ways of the established order, very much as a dog is trained to obey its master. For some reason, more inscrutable than meets the eye, their own teaching is above this kind of "training," evidently because radical critique is so pure and precious that it can only be of a "higher" order. Yet, if they were to practice what they preach to its logical conclusion, if they were really to take in earnest their belief that the teaching of political science is itself a political act, they would introduce into the curriculum those techniques of radical political action that found their way into the curriculum of some of the late "free universities," such as the fine art of what was called "trashing," the home-made fabrication of Molotov cocktails, or the noble practice of disrupting the lectures of those whose ideas are counter to their own noble ends. It is perhaps to the credit of most self-styled radical teachers that they are unwilling to take this route, though many of them, one had occasion to observe some years ago, also refused to interpose their bodies when misguided students drew the understandable conclusion that radical critique without radical action could only be considered hypocritical.

The Proposition need not *per se* entail these violent aberrations from the mission of education. By the same token, however, one cannot take as self-evident the opposite allegation—that dispassionate and disinterested teaching and scholarship conduce to political complacency and quietism. One need not be a barn-burner to be politically concerned. The Proposition has no ethical merit and deserves to be rejected as being alien to the vocation of the teacher of political science.

The Moral Argument—Of Right and Wrong

If the teaching of political science were itself a political act, what would be the moral implications of the teacher's conduct as a political actor? Raising the moral question makes sense only if the Proposition is not found acceptable. Otherwise—because the Proposition postulates that the teacher is and should be an actor in behalf of one or more *particular* political values or causes to the exclusion of others—there would be no moral issue. For a moral issue can only be said to exist if there is a problem, a dilemma, or a conflict of conscience whose resolution requires a choice among alternatives. The ideologue has no such conflict of conscience. Because he believes in the essential correctness of his own intellectual posture as a matter beyond question or doubt, he is not willing to suspend judgment even for a moment in order to examine, not to say neutralize, the bias involved in his position; on the contrary, he will defend the propagation of bias as the appropriate educational strategy.

If the morality of an "ethic of ultimate ends" is *in abstracto* amoral, it becomes forthrightly unmoral in the educational situation. For in this situation teacher and student do not meet on terms of equality. By virtue of his role as a trustee of esoteric knowledge, as an "authority" on matters of political science and philosophy to which he has given long and careful study, the teacher is in possession of something not possessed by the student. Although it is one of his obligations to share his knowledge with the student, the teacher is placed in a superior position vis-à-vis the student which, unless restrained, can easily become one of domination and exploitation. In due time, the student may become the teacher's peer in knowledge. In the short run—and most educational encounters are short run—the student is in fact at the teacher's mercy. It therefore behooves the teacher to be most circumspect not only in regard to how he teaches but also what he teaches. The moral teacher will show the student what his intellectual options are, and he will give him the opportunity to choose among these options.

The teaching of political science, then, like all teaching, is nothing less than an exercise in self-restraint. This exercise is a moral exercise because, precisely if one does not subscribe to the Proposition, the teacher carries an enormous responsibility. It is a truly moral exercise because it involves the making of difficult choices—what to include in a course of study and what to exclude, what to emphasize as significant or insignificant, what to praise and what to condemn, what to demand of the student and what not to demand, what to judge good work and what bad, and so on and so forth. In the teaching situation enlightened by the "ethics of responsibility," the neutralization of bias is not only a functional requisite of free scholarly inquiry but also a moral imperative. It is, moreover, not the only imperative that defines the teacher's role. Unless the educational situation be one of fraud and deception, it requires full disclosure of just those criteria that underlie the processes of elimination and selection in the choice of lecture topics or reading materials. One could add further imperatives, but these will suffice to demonstrate why the Proposition violates the worth and dignity of the student. It is a maxim that, in effect, has been invoked all too often to sanctify the teacher's domination of the student's mind in the name of God, Country, Leader, or Ideology. It is, in the perspective of a liberal humanism, a thoroughly discredited and discreditable proposition.

Now, if the Proposition meant that education in political science is a moral act, and if the political were also the moral, one could hardly object. But what in a given interpersonal relationship is moral and what political does not coincide, and such coincidence is not really assumed in the Proposition. On the contrary, the Proposition is nothing less than a justification for violating the moral order which normally regulates the teacher-student relationship. Rather than expanding the teacher's as well as the student's options in making intellectual and political choices, treating political science education as a political act restricts these choices and justifies an unmorality that can only be destructive of genuine political education.

Political science education as a political act would not only commit that education to a given ideological "line," whether imposed by the teacher on his own volition or on pressure from the interests to whom he may be beholden; it would also seek to enforce the line counter to proper educational morality. At its worst, the Proposition justifies the communication of false or partial knowledge, the withholding of knowledge, the suppression of criticism, the punishment of deviant students, and so on. For the task of political science education would be to indoctrinate and not to educate.

There is, however, another "moral lesson" that might be read into the Proposition. Assuming that the Proposition truly states the educational situation, and that the student-teacher relationship lends itself to domination and exploitation, the only morally justifiable solution would seem to lie in the "democratization" of teaching and learning. Students and teachers should meet only as equals; teachers should be "responsive" to student wishes; and students should participate in decisions as to what is to be taught and how to teach it. The learning situation so constructed would be a true "community" in the best sense of being a moral order.

This vision of educational organization is evidently predicated on the rather naive assumption that democratization would make the "political" in the Proposition something less of an objectionable stigma. What in this conception makes political science education evidently obnoxious is not that it is a political act but that it is not "democratic." The only way to "liberate" education about politics from its coercive shackles is through introducing into it even more politics, but a politics of a kind which will be "right" because itself determined by majoritarian or other "democratic" techniques.

There is something morally attractive in this scent of utopia but, on reflection, it is as unmoral as the alleged political order in education which it seeks to replace. My concern here is not the impracticality of this utopian version of teaching about politics, but the violence it does to teaching as a profession. For it postulates that knowledge and truth about political things can be ascertained by political edict or decision. It in fact deprives the teacher not only of his authority but also of his autonomy as a creative person. What is to be taught is to be determined by majoritarian vote of all those involved in the educational system (conceivably including not only students but also administrators and those who pay the bill). The teacher is no longer obligated to the canons of scholarship but subject to the whims and fancies of forever shifting factions and coalitions. He either becomes a political actor who, through bargaining and compromise, will seek to protect what little autonomy he may be able to squeeze out of the game of educational politics; or he becomes a political merchant eager to please his customers by selling them what they want or by huckstering what the consumers neither need nor really want.

There is something inherently unmoral in this conception of political science teaching as a political act, even though it is, and indeed because it is, given an aura of "democratic" justification. The teacher who willingly surrenders his authority and autonomy as a man of learning to the fleeting predilections of the passing multitude of students and other consumers of knowledge is as unmoral as the teacher who exploits the protected educational environment by imposing his own political or ideological predilections on an unsuspecting and only all too innocent student body.

The teacher of political science need not be either arbitrary master or supplicant slave. His moral posture vis-à-vis his students should be that of the person of learning who may not know all there is to know, but whose knowledge presumably places him in a better position to discriminate between student wants and needs than students themselves are able to do. One may concede that students may know better than the teacher what they want, but what they want is not necessarily the same thing as what they need. And while the teacher may not know what students want, he should presumably know what they need by way of an education. If this were not so, then it would make little sense to distinguish between student and teacher.

It is easy to see why there should be a good deal of confusion in this respect, for the psychological borderline between wants and needs is both zigzag and poorly marked. This is precisely the reason why the political science teacher's morality cannot be political, whatever meaning one may give the term. On the contrary, because he must steer a dangerous course between what students want and what they need by way of knowledge, his position is an eminently moral one.

Lest I be misunderstood, let me say, though it should be needless to say, that I am not equating education with morality and politics with unmorality. What I am talking about is the mission of education in political science which, like the mission of political practice, may be moral or unmoral. Whether education or politics is moral or unmoral is always a matter of the ethical assumption that underlies one's moral judgments as well as a matter of empirical determination in a given instance. But I hope to have shown that if, as is proposed, the teaching of political science were itself to be a political act, it could only be an unmoral act.

Conclusion: Return to the Studio

Let me return to the analogy of the difference between the studio and the forum. Perhaps I have ventured too far, beyond the limits that one should set to the political in scholarly discourse about political education. Perhaps this paper is a positive demonstration of the Proposition that "the teaching of political science is itself a political act." Hopefully it is a demonstration of something else: that the scholar in his studio can have an open view on the world of politics, indeed that he can have political views, without becoming a political activist.

The studio, wherever it is, is the place where the scholar feels at home. In the studio he can be truly comfortable with himself because he can be truly honest with himself in what he thinks and says. In the studio alone neither political ambition nor political pretense interferes with the pursuit of knowledge.

The classroom is an extension of the studio and not of the forum. The forum is a place the student of politics should visit often and which he should come to know thoroughly; and his participation in the forum as a citizen or politician should enrich his scholarly potential. But he can only learn *from* the forum and cannot learn *in* the forum, for the forum is an arena of political action and not of scholarship. If the scholar were to act in the classroom as those act whom he observes in the forum—partisans, propagandists, lobbyists, politicians, ideologues, and so on—he would no longer remain true to his calling. Being a warrior in the combats of the forum is a role for which the scholar or teacher is neither trained nor qualified. It is for this reason that the classroom cannot be a replica of the forum, for the teacher of politics is taught to teach and not conduct political business. The task of education in political science is and must be fundamentally different from the function of politics in society.

The notion of the classroom as an extension of the studio deserves elaboration, but I must leave discussion to another occasion. Suffice it to say that the classroom, like the studio, is a place not for the execution but for the germination of ideas, not for their propagation but for their testing in the light of reason and evidence. If the classroom is treated as a forum of political action and not as a studio of disinterested scholarship, the educational process is aborted before it can begin. There is and should be an open and easy passage from studio through the classroom to the forum, and a way back. For it is the task of political science to bring the raw materials of politics into the studio and into the classroom, to subject them to analysis and synthesis, to create knowledge of political things and transmit it to students. This is what Weber had in mind when he wrote that "ideas occur to us when they please, not when it pleases us." But, he continued, "ideas would certainly not come to mind had we not brooded at our desks and searched for answers with passionate devotion." The classroom, like the studio, should be sacrosanct as an island of creative or critical thought and not become a forum of political action or decision.

FOOTNOTES

*This paper was written while I was a scholar in residence at the Villa Serbelloni, the Study and Conference Center of the Rockefeller Foundation in Bellagio, Italy, during August, 1974.

1. The following paragraph is an all too brief summary of a paper I wrote several years ago. See "Values and Behavioral Science: Neutrality Revisited," in Heinz Eulau, *Micro-Macro Political Analysis* (Chicago: Aldine Publishing Company, 1969), pp. 364-369.

2. Sheldon Wolin, "Political Theory as a Vocation," in Martin Fleisher, ed., *Machiavelli and the Nature of Political Thought* (New York: Atheneum Publishers, 1972), p. 69.

3. *Ibid.*, p. 71. I am aware of quoting out of context. Wolin's argument is more subtle and complex than can be revealed by a couple of quotes.

4. I do not know what Wolin means by "official political science." It seems to refer to all tendencies in political science that he dislikes, but especially to what he calls "methodism." Wolin's essay is a sophisticated but highly biased vendetta against those who have faith in the possibility of a science of politics. It is the kind of "teaching" (if read by students) that is inimical to the values of scholarship: it does, indeed, make the teaching of political science a political act, for he wants it to be that way.

CHAPTER 4

The Classroom and Political Science: An Essay on Political Theory

MARTIN LANDAU
University of California
Berkeley

I

Participation in a conference on teaching political science is a pleasure: especially when its prospectus instructs that "inquiry into questions relating to teaching is an important intellectual enterprise." I have always believed that the classroom is pre-eminently a scholarly situation, that its stock-in-trade is knowledge, and that it should aspire to a scientific status. Accordingly, I take the suggestion that teaching is a political act to be the height of nonsense and would dismiss such a claim out of hand were it not for the fact that it constitutes so dangerous a doctrine. I am of the generation that associates this position with the principle of *senatus consultum*—a principle that found such vivid and tragic expression from "Moscow to the Mediterranean" in the decades before the Great War and, alas, still finds adherents.

The American version has, fortunately, been relatively mild—probably because of the system's pluralism. But the doctrine itself has been pressed by a variety of forces, in different ways, at different times and places and in varying degrees of intensity. This is not the place to engage in a history of academic freedom but it is clear to all of us that there are elements outside of the academy that have always pressed to hold faculties *politically* accountable. They range from vigilantes, through boards of trustees, to legislative committees and the editorial pages of our press. No surprise is engendered when the doctrine emanates from such sources.

The anomaly appears when it is given credence within the university. I first encountered it as an undergraduate student at a time when ideological discussion raged throughout the campus. As a graduate student, I again experienced it, however subtly, in the reaction to Herbert Simon's heretical construction of the concept of decision on what has now become an infamous disjunction, the fact-value dichotomy—an act for which many have never forgiven him. In the ensuing years, the doctrine has regularly cropped up in symposia on "great issues," in APSA committees on teaching, in tracts on citizenship training, in debates over undergraduate—even graduate—curricula, and in a good deal of our confused writings on philosophy and public policy. Now we face it most directly in the anti-text-books of the moment, conservative and radical; it has been an issue in association conflict; and it has been pressed by many colleagues whose vocation is normative theory. Provoked by the tragic and disillusioning events of the last decade, and prompted by a terrible sense of urgency, they have sought to right wrong and do good. But I am afraid that if the notion that teaching is a political act was to be successfully established, it would—at the very least—return us to that period in American education which historians refer to as "the theological era"—a time when the test of a theory was held to be the morality of the theorist: today, of course, it would be the politics of the theorist.

Whatever the altruism that moves this doctrine, my studies have convinced me that it is directed against the scientific movement in social science—and in no small measure. In some instances, it is more to be seen as a counterstroke to science than an effort to eliminate injustice and chicane.

I recall a protest meeting called by students immediately after the revelation of the Cambodian "incursion." They were, like most of us then, profoundly disturbed and deeply distressed. There were a variety of speakers, all of whom addressed this latest abomination of the administration—some powerfully and cogently, quite a few hysterically. There was one speaker, however—a graduate student in political theory—who shall ever remain memorable. After an impassioned denunciation of the Nixon-Kissinger duplicity, he excoriated a "value-free" political science to then arrive at his master stroke: "Once and for all," he declared, "we must destroy the fact-value dichotomy."

I do not now find this as ridiculous as it first appeared to me. For the insistence that teaching (and research) is a political act has to be predicated on the notion that there can only be the most tenuous separation between a statement of value and a statement of fact—if there is any at all. The argument today is no different than that which

mistakenly but successfully placed the politics-administration dichotomy in dispute. It is not that sentences which express values are facts,
it is that all synthetic statements are so constrained by values as to
render the difference negligible. It follows then that objectivity in the
social sciences is a myth—if not a cunning ruse. To pursue it is to
pursue a phantom, and to abdicate from our social responsibilities as
citizens and as scholars. It is on this basis that one finds a demand for
relevance that is to be expressed through an activist spirit engaged in
the pursuit of "affirmative goals."

The sound of this phrase is mellifluous: and, frankly, I like affirmative goals better than negative goals. But even this concept troubles me when I approach it in the context of contemporary criticism.
For some, too many in my estimate, affirmation has meant "an end to
political science" and its replacement by a *political* political science—
which makes some sense if all of our propositions are and can only
be valuational. Or it has meant that our classrooms are to become
therapeutic in character—a stance which has transformed many of
them into encounter (and sensitivity training) groups. In the main,
however, it is associated with normative considerations: with what
is now called normative theory—which, it is hoped, will provide new
directions, new visions and dreams, and a proper ordering of our
preferences.

Normative theory, as I understand this concept, is concerned
exclusively with value judgments—with evaluative predicates as distinguished from descriptive predicates. It tells what ought to be, not
what is. It makes value judgments. It says what is good and what is
bad, what is worthy and unworthy, what is right and wrong. It tells
us how we should live: and is not in any way invalidated because we
don't follow its injunctions. Those who insist that there is no tenable
distinction between fact and value need to consider the status of a
descriptive formulation when it is observed that we do not behave
in accordance with its predications. "Men should not lie" is not rendered false by a liar: "Men do not lie" is.

It is also of interest that normative theory tends not to say very
much about the properties of values: while it tells us what kinds of
behaviors are good, the explication of the concept itself is generally
left to meta-normative inquiry which, it may surprise some, does not
make value judgments. It is in the latter domain that the status of a
value is held to be problematical—its meaning, usage, and justification

are the critical elements here. There is, thus, one dimension of normative inquiry that is not value-laden and yet is crucial to all normative discourse since it turns on the explication of such concepts as goodness, virtue, and value itself—and the procedures to be employed to warrant them. Any examination of this literature makes it abundantly clear that it is not an easy task to clarify or define the term "value."[1]

II

That there is a large place for normative considerations in a classroom is, in my view, beyond doubt. But this neither necessitates the introduction of a party line nor the rejection of strictly scientific canons. On the contrary, the normative problems that we daily confront require the hardest kind of knowledge for their resolution; which is to say, as I want to show below, that in this world it takes a good deal of knowledge to be a moral man. It is not only that the road to hell is paved with good intentions but, as Henry Jones Ford once observed, no mark of wisdom is to be assigned to those who mistake reverie for thought and feeling for judgment—nor is it very helpful to impute to our projects the merit of their motives.

To place the general problem of "the teacher and the polity" in some historical perspective, I shall not return to Aristotle. I would much rather call attention to Morris Raphael Cohen's *Reason and Nature*. Published in 1931, its first chapter, written in the mid-twenties, opens as follows:

> Despite the frequent assertion that ours is the age of science, we are witnessing today a remarkably widespread decline of the prestige of intellect and reason. . . . Even among professed philosophers, the high priests of the sanctuary of reason, faith in rational or demonstrative science is systematically being minimized in the interests of "practical" idealism, vitalism, humanism, intuitionism, and other forms of avowed anti-intellectualism. . . .
>
> There can be little doubt that this distrust of reason has its roots deep in the dominant temper of our age, an age whose feverish restlessness makes it impatiently out of tune with the slow rhythm of deliberate order. The art, literature, and politics of Europe and of our own country show an ever-growing contempt for ideas and form . . . , attaching

greater value to novel impressions and vehement expression than to coherency and order. The romantic or "Dionysiac" contempt for prudence and deliberative (so-called bourgeois) morality is a crude expression of the same reaction against scientific or rigorous intellectual procedure,—a reaction which makes our modern illuminati like Bergson and Croce dismiss physical science as devoid of any genuine knowledge. . . . It would preposterously exaggerate the actual influence of philosophy if the outrageously shameless contempt for truth shown in the various forms of recent propaganda were attributed to the systematic scorn heaped by modernistic philosophies on the old ideal of the pursuit of truth for its own sake "in scorn of consequences." Yet this decline of respect for truth in public or national affairs is certainly not devoid of all significant connection with its decline in philosophy and art.

Forty odd years later, the temptation to state that history repeats itself is great. But in my memory bank, there are some bits which refer to Munro's "laws of the pendulum." And despite my hesitation in employing metaphoric transfers, there does seem to be something cyclical in our concern with values.

I know that I risk scorn in some quarters, but since I have referred to Simon, I might as well use his formula in dealing with this question. I shall probably be less than successful, but I may make a point.

The original model centers on the concept of decision, defined as a choice on the basis of a set of valuational and factual premises. While these are treated as analytically and epistemologically distinct, both types of premises are (by definition) present in every decision. Where, however, a decision leads to the selection of final goals, it may be treated as a value judgment. I wish to rephrase this as follows: where in a choice set facts are either held constant or bracketed, i.e. when the value premise predominates, the decision is to be taken as a matter of values—as a value judgment. And, conversely, where values are bracketed (held constant) the decision is to be taken as a matter of fact—as a technical judgment. Value premises that are intermediate in a means-end chain are thereby transformed into empirical questions.

The unit of analysis is the *premise*: and the thrust of the model is the analysis of the premises upon which decisions are based. Simon, of course, began the task of formalizing this model, but it has been in wide use for a long time in political science—a use, however, which has generally been informal in character. Inquiry into the source, content and character of decision premises reaches back, in the modern discipline, to our first studies of economic determinism (J. Allen Smith—1907; Charles A. Beard—1908), of psychological motivation (Graham Wallas—1908), and to Arthur Bentley's work despite his insistence that the unit of analysis must be the group (Bentley—1908). Since then there has developed an enormous literature that has attempted to establish the effects on decision premises of such factors as ideology, culture, social class, the family, peer groups, reference groups, personality structure and more, with studies of socialization seeking to describe the process through which these influences have been impressed. In fact, *all* of our studies of political behavior are, implicitly or otherwise, centrally concerned with the decision premise. And the entire effort has been constituted as a descriptive enterprise: it has been entered upon as a strictly empirical venture, motivated by the value-goals of a veridical knowledge.

There are those, however, who have insisted that political science must be primarily, even exclusively, normative in character. That its central task is the evaluation of political life, the formulation and generation of basic, intrinsic, values, and their promotion and inculcation. Such values, to be sure, have been bracketed in the empirical venture: in the normative undertaking the opposite tends to be the case. A tension between the two positions marks our history—and debate and conflict have turned on which set of premises shall control our direction—descriptive or evaluative. We seem, in direct response to the state of community at large, to have cycled between the two.

In stable periods, community politics at all levels engages in what may be seen as a form of "stationary engineering and design." It disregards the parametric features of the system by bracketing basic values, thereby rendering them non-problematic. It tends to be absorbed by technical or factual matters and turns attention toward the improvement of the internal operation of the system. It will move to mount reform programs, to eliminate shocking discrepancies and anomalies, to make the system more efficient, but basic systemic values remain unchallenged. In such periods, motivational unity is generally assumed and the concept of neutrality—as in the merit system—flourishes. Nor is much attention paid to the university except as an invaluable source of technical expertise.

At other times, say the depression era, the direction changes. Concern centers on "system design" itself and parameters, once so nicely bracketed, become the *decisive* elements of contention. Deep rifts open, and intense struggles occur over basic principles, values, and goals. The community is torn by bitter and protracted ideological struggle—and neutrality ceases to be a desirable property. Inside the university, the same rifts appear, and conflict over disciplinary purposes revives. Demonstrative science is systematically minimized in the interest of practical idealism and humanism, and of ideology. While outside, survival is said to be the issue. In such circumstances motivational unity cannot be assumed. It is to be secured. The academy itself becomes problematical and it is not too difficult to sanction head-hunting—only it was then known as red-hunting. This reached a startling climax in the infamous McCarthy period when adherence to a specified set of valuational premises became a condition of all public office—and the warrant for secular excommunication. It was called the loyalty program.

In the decade following the mid-fifties, the circumstances eased. We were stable. We had full-employment and the greatest stock market in history. It was an era of good feeling—in which it was proclaimed that America had seen the end of ideology. Back we go to stationary planning and with our parameters beyond question we again unlimber a high technology to make the system ever more efficient. The conflict in the discipline eases as does conflict in the community.

Life, however, often confounds our deepest wishes and I need not recite the events that have turned this cycle around. Nor need I carry this through the New Political Science, the New Public Administration, the post-behavioral revolution—and the systematic scorn that has been heaped on the old ideal of the pursuit of truth for its own sake—a pursuit that takes modern form as a search and research for valid factual premises.

But I must emphasize that the invention of the hypothesis is one of the great liberating forces of the modern world. It is worth reminding ourselves that the legitimacy of factual premises in public decision-making, in politics, was an epochal problem in the development of western society. Once upon a time, institutions were ordered on the basis of arbitrary and *infallible* authority. The practical-empirical knowledge of the day was passed along as custom and tradition, warranted and sustained on sacred grounds. Discrepancies and anomalies were dealt with scholastically, and if they could not be fitted to the categories of the sacred system, they were exorcised as heresy and sin. Societies of this kind do not admit of the hypothesis: their decision rules are essentially, dogmatically, matters of value.

The hold weakened during the Renaissance but it was the English empiricists who declared war on dogma. The enemy was revealed truth, the claim to "inspired infallibility," and "principles that must not be questioned." The thrust was directed against the subordination of experience to dogma. The *tabula rasa* was offered as one solution to the question—from where does knowledge come? "To this I (John Locke) answer, in one word, from experience; in that all knowledge is founded, and from that it ultimately derives itself." The science of Bacon, the materialism of Hobbes, the empiricism of Locke, and the discoveries of Newton—all laid the basis for the admission of empirical premises into the public decision process. Nor was the effort to establish the legitimacy of such premises a simple and unobstructed succession of victories—even to recent times. There were we recall, hypotheses—no, heresies: the Copernican reversal of planetary position was indexed, denounced as false and profane doctrine. Bruno was excommunicated and burned: and Galileo the telescope-maker could not get his Inquisitors to look through its lens. Centuries later, but long before the Scopes trial, Oliver Wendell Holmes would insist that the life of the law is experience. And his friend would plead with our highest court to admit empirical premises into their decision system. This was the point of the "Brandeis brief."

Such efforts were designed to liberate the mind of man. In their long march, they transformed sin into error and thereby increased by orders of magnitude the "allowable area" of choice. The movement was anything but anti-humane.

There seems now to be a terrible fear that the scientific mode demands that we apologize for feeling: that its rigorous rules of rationality are anti-humanist in spirit—displacing substantive rationality and therefore the primacy of values. Apart from the usual spate of charges—triviality, irrelevance, and the like, it is said to constitute an approach that depreciates politics, curtails the domain of democratic decision-making and the control that we must exercise over the choice set.

In societies so complex as those we inhabit, we do face dilemmas of monumental proportions. That we continually confront the triumph of technique over purpose, or the displacement of goals is beyond challenge. But to attribute this to the analytic-synthetic distinction, to the difference in epistemological status between a value and a fact, is certainly to be challenged. There is nothing in this decision rule which necessarily or pragmatically mandates either goal displacement or the dulling of our moral sensibilities. On the contrary, to assign a decision to the category "good" requires knowledge. This is especially the case in modern society, characterized as it is by endless and complex means-end chains which exhibit the property of increasing uncertainty (the absorption of uncertainty) and magnification of error potential. We need to emphasize that any decision along this chain stands as a hypothesis—the validation of which can only be established by observation of the chain reaction it produces. That is, whether or not a decision constitutes a satisfactory (good) solution of the problem which originally prompted it, can only be determined on the basis of its immediate, intermediate, and long range effects. The fact that we frequently have to contend with "unanticipated consequences" is a sign that we fall far short of the knowledge we need.

Accordingly, to *value* a decision requires a knowledge that permits us to fit choices to a problem as we fit medicine to a disease. Without bothering at this point to open the elusive question of ultimate values, it should be apparent that the development of science, whatever difficulties it has generated, has increased the number of "choice sets" open to us, as well as the range of alternatives in each. The growth of knowledge bestows upon us a greater freedom of choice by providing us with an ever-increasing repertoire of response. It expands the fund of goal alternatives available to select from. And the elevation of factual premises in our decision system serves to increase the probability that those we select will be relevant and satisfactory solutions to the problems we seek to solve. Science does not demand an apology for feeling: it demands that we shall not apologize for thinking.

Unhappily, however, it is the affective mode that is upon us and its idiom is poetic. It talks of expressive behavior and the creation of visions—and of realities. The hope is for self-actualization, authenticity of relationship, and a novel and extended consciousness. At the last annual meeting of APSA, I participated in a two-session panel devoted to paradigmatic problems in public administration. I was the seventh speaker of eight and when my turn came I found myself, almost reflexively, opening my statement with the declaration that my style is cognitive, not affective. And this because several of my colleagues were, on the authority of the Book of Kuhn, delivering sermons on the religious aspects of theories and models, while others were concerned to release my inhibitions and free my psyche. But all of this paled before a session of the previous day.

Unknowingly, in sublime ignorance of what was to come, I had agreed to chair a panel devoted to "Metaphor, Image and Paradigm as Foundation for Political Theory." Our first speaker was—indeed he was—an autonomous man. In the majesty of unrestrained emotion and honesty of self he bared his breast—fully: which was probably a wise choice since there was more in the breast than the head. Proclaiming that he was "me, myself and I, standing—here and now," he delivered several of the many aphorisms of which his paper is composed. Truth, he tells us, is a stench in the burnt out ghetto of his mind. This "general truth" (for that is what an aphorism embodies) followed immediately, in the same short section, upon the imperative "Political theory should be poetry": after all, Aristotle had written a *Politics* and a *Poetics*: he did not write a *Politics* and a *Statistics*.

And if poetry does not suffice then the play is the thing. A second fellow, much more considered in his remarks, turned us "towards a sketch of dramaturgy" on the basis of the "Artistic Foundations for Political Space." A third fellow did trigger my emotions but these remained unexpressed: his shouting intimidated me. Not so a good part of our participating audience, however. "Becoming Political," theatrically in search of their definitive selves, easily transcending necessity, and so very existential, they were anything but playful. For a while, there, I was uncertain as to where I was. There is no question about it: it went beyond mere mundane (earthly) experience. After a time, the scene shifted when several exasperated people began to address Flathman's discussion of Winch and Wittgenstein. I felt then that I was back on earth.

It is, without doubt, entirely legitimate to think and write in many idioms—and I am not ready to close off any, believing as I do that redundant channels are invaluable, and that no one must be permitted to block the way of inquiry. Nor, in my view, is it to be doubted that resistance to dogma requires the constant creation of what are now called "new visions"—which we used to refer to as new ideas. Poetry and drama—thoughtful, imaginative, creative—often supply us with hints and clues, even with a new reality, as they say. In my own inquiry, this is not a term that I am prone to use but I am ready to entertain the claim that a ruling class creates our reality; that there are multiple realities; that we've got to change our reality—to make it and control it. I must also say that while much of what I've read on this subject is, in the greatest measure, either obscurantist or illogical, I remain mindful of Huxley's warning that there is no greater mistake than the hasty conclusion that opinions are worthless because they are poorly argued.

But I am baffled by proposals that are predicated on the assumption that new visions and new realities are beyond a scientific reach. How, indeed, can anyone tell the story of science and exclude from his-story the countless number of "realities" that have been proffered. Not all stick, however, for science is not a fairy tale. This is Whitehead's injunction: and we must understand it to refer to the way the scientific mode of analysis takes visions, treats them as possibilities (for which term one may correctly substitute "theories"), and then seeks to transform them into probabilities. So it is that there is a world of microorganisms, of electrons and protons, of genes and chromosomes, and of spiral nebulae—billions of such galaxies, and island universes—which "realities" have corrected, constantly so, our erroneous notions of the real stuff of nature. And in the social sciences we have created the subconscious and the unconscious, exchanges and coalitions, classes and ideologies, bureaucracies and polyarchies, and we have ranged from a micro-politics to that of whole systems; all of which and more have been offered to us as the real stuff of political life.

Theorists, normative and empirical, do share one property with poets: they provide us with images. And so does science. And philosophy. There is a caveat, however, which I take once again from Morris Cohen:

> Philosophy is primarily a vision and all great philosophers have something in common with the poets and the prophets. But while vision, intuition, or wisdom is the substance of any philosophy that is worthwhile, serious philosophy must also be something more than a poetic image or prophecy. It must, like science, be also vitally concerned with reasoned or logically demonstrable truth. Granted that great truths begin as poetic or prophetic insights, it still remains true that the views of poets and prophets have in fact often proved narrowly one-sided, conflicting, incoherent, and illusory. To introduce

order and consistency into our vision, to remove pleasing but illusory plausibilities by contrasting various views with their possible alternatives, and to judge critically all pretended proofs in the light of the most rigorously logical rules of evidence, is the indispensable task of any serious philosophy. The seed which ripens into vision may be a gift of the gods but the labor of cultivating it so that it may bear nourishing fruit is the indispensable function of arduous scientific technique.

III

It is my belief that we require more of the scientific spirit in our classrooms: that the work which is there engaged in is not sufficiently objective—a conclusion that I draw from our textbooks.

My reference to objectivity should not be taken to mean neutrality; or a divine ability to "excise value judgments and policy preferences" from either our teaching or our writing. It is rather lamentable that discussions of *objectivity* continually and erroneously make this concept a synonym of *neutrality*—establishing as its equivalent the notion of a value-free scientist. That this is done is ironic: for it is the fact that objectivity in science is equated with the quite contrary assumption that all observers are biased. I have pursued this problem at some length elsewhere[2] and I do not wish to restate the full argument here. But some remarks are in order.

In the scientific universe of discourse, the idea of a perfectly neutral actor is pure fiction and the quest for such an actor is deemed a fool's errand. Indeed, it is precisely the recognition of the insurmountable difficulties involved in attaining neutrality that has generated the system of regulation that is called "objectivity."

The crux of this concept should be rather familiar to political scientists: it is Madisonian in character. It rests on the prime assumption that men, even scientific men, are not angels; that they are not and cannot be infallible. None are value-free and all are prone to error: they are, simply stated, risky actors. Because there is certainly more to seeing than meets the eyeball, because we are ideologically and culturally constrained, because there is no such phenomenon as immaculate perception, all claims that are tendered must be subject to rigorous error correcting procedures. These take form as a system of powerful, redundant, and visible external and independent checks —from which there is granted no immunity and no exemption whatsoever. There are no privileged claims in science and there are no privileged persons. In the realm of cognition, therefore, *objectivity is not and cannot be a personal property*. It is, rather, an *institutionalized control system* that is designed to hold every claim accountable. The principle of accountability of assertion, not neutrality, marks the concept of objectivity.

These control procedures—the indispensable function of arduous scientific technique—are themselves determined by the nature of the assertions we advance, by the properties of a theory, a hypothesis, a finding, or even a policy—as I shall show below. Because they lay claims against experience, experience itself must play the role of independent controller and impartial arbiter. When reference is made to the debates that presently engage philosophers and scientists on this question, it usually fails to notice that contemporary controversies turn on the never ending quest to find ever more effective regulators. The concept of independent empirical check, e.g., is in process of being refined so as to comprehend a system of criticism that rests on strong alternative theories. Here we may point to a growing insistence, prompted by a continuous examination of methods of accountability, that even the most well-confirmed theory is to be perpetually challenged. The enemy is dogma, for it is guaranteed to produce error. Strong alternatives, strong competitors, provide an additional or redundant criticism that may even be sharper than the comparison of the original theory with the domain of experience it orders: for they can produce contrary evidence which the original theory failed to uncover.

The concept of objectivity instructs that a system cannot be scientific unless and until it is set on the principle of external independent checks, on the foundation of rigorous criticism.

The incident that I now want to relate happened early in my teaching career. The place was Brooklyn College, which—as you may know—housed an intellectually elite student body. Loaded with a good measure of the conceit that is a general academic property, I was "giving" an elective in American politics. The course rolled along nicely: I had organized it carefully, the reading list was full, the students were interested, they read the assignments, and participated in discussion. I felt pretty good. My introductory classes had done well on the standard departmental exam, and my elective mid-terms were excellent.

In that class, there was only one irritation—a student who, from the second week on, just looked through the window. One day I asked if anything was troubling him. His response, "Yes, your entire analysis is wrong." Why, I ask. I'm not sure, he replies: it just doesn't ring right. Well, I say rather cavalierly, when you find out, let me know. And I continue to roll along. Thereafter he fails to appear in class and as time passes, I prepare an F for him: he misses the midterm, doesn't show for a make-up, tells me that my analysis is entirely wrong, and then disappears. Great. On the last day of the term he presents himself. Arriving late, probably deliberately so—it was a grand entrance—he walked to the desk, dropped a thick manuscript before me and in a loud voice announced, "This, sir, is why you are wrong." It is possible my belief that the study of error is the best introduction to the search for truth—and the best pedagogy we can employ—began at this moment.[3]

We tend to routinize our classes, and our students tend to be routineers. We structure our courses too completely, we syllabus them too fully, we provide complete bibliographies—and we tend thereby to treat a class as a closed set of variables. In the language of decision-theory, we prematurely program, and this leads to our own form of Gresham's law: easy decisions drive out difficult ones as easy problems drive out the hard. The hard are a function of mind, the easy a function of memory. When recitation substitutes for analysis, our students become walking card-catalogues. They are that even if we call them erudite.

Today, alas, a new twist has been added, for it is feelings that are to substitute for analysis. Hence the pedagogy of transcendental encounter and occupational therapy. Here the thrust is to employ sympathy and empathy as the explanatory variable—making it rather predictable that affective predicates will soon exhaust our vocabulary.

In contrast to this, I want to *know* the warrants for belief. I want to *know* the ground which sustains an assertion. I want my students to ask such questions—of me, of themselves, of our textbooks, and of our theories. I do not want any busywork: I am not in the business of constructing endurance contests. I want them to be ever sensitive to error, to values disguised as facts, to tautologies presented as hypotheses, and to the way in which persuasive definitions predispose us to confuse a theory with the phenomena it points to. They must be alert to the fallacy of reification, to the error potential of the everyday sampling that we engage in and call "impression," and to "dangerous hypotheses."[4] And they must learn the difficulties involved in addressing an extensional world through the medium of intensional terms.

I want all of this and more in the spirit of scientific criticism: not *ad hominem*, but in accordance with the principle of accountability of assertion. "We do not believe any group of men adequate enough or wise enough to operate without scrutiny or without criticism," Oppenheimer once wrote. "We know that the only way to avoid error is to detect it, and the only way to detect is to be free to inquire."

Freedom of inquiry permits, if it does not encourage, the "recognition of possibilities." Hence it is that students must also be pressed to create and develop hypotheses and theories when confronted with surprise. Their task is invention, not recitation—the invention of solutions to puzzling problems. It is frequently the case that I examine students by asking them to invent a theory to explain an anomaly. But I also want them to understand that *a theory which cannot be refuted under any circumstance, which is so constructed as to make refutation impossible, presents itself as a privileged claim*: or, as the biologist W. A. Rushton once put it, "if a theory cannot be mortally endangered, it is not alive."

IV

My final comment has to do with the place of values in the classroom—which, in my scheme of things, is not different from their place in science.

The notion abounds that scientific inquiry must stop at the threshold of values. Nothing could be further from the truth. It is the case that scientific procedures cannot warrant basic, ultimate, intrinsic, or nonderivative values. And that is because of their epistemological status: they do not stand as descriptive predicates and, therefore, cannot be held accountable in the same manner as an empirical claim. How we hold them accountable, how we show them to be false—depends. It depends on whether we are intuitionists, naturalists, emotivists, theologists—and the many subsets of these categories. The justification of a non-derivative value is a baffling enterprise—varying with whether we are cognitivists or not. In ordinary life we usually avoid the problem by resorting to the doctrine "*de gustibus non est dis-*

putandum"—a favored stratagem of both barbers and jurists. On too many occasions, however, efforts are made to coerce acceptance of such values; in such an event the rule of justification is clear—"might makes right."

But the normative problems that present themselves to us do not take this form exclusively. From time to time, they do occupy our attention, but it is more likely that the value judgments we confront are elliptical and, therefore, intermediate. In fact, most come to us as grading acts, prescriptions, and the like. In this circumstance, we can deal with them quite objectively, for they will be either derivative or empirical in character.

If they are derivative, then the problem we face in normative theory is axiological. The questions that have to be raised turn on the consistency of belief—on whether or not they have been properly deduced. A derivative value entails a prior value: prior values are necessarily presupposed. We can, therefore, inquire into the logic, the mode of reasoning, that produced a particular derivation. In this sense, axiological inquiry serves the same function in normative theory as methodology does in empirical theory. It is a check against error. Accordingly, there is every reason to scrutinize values carefully—especially in a domain that abounds with inconsistent, elliptical, and ambiguous ideological and normative formulations. And if one accepts the concept of decision that I have employed, such error checks can only serve to clarify the value premises that enter into our decision-making and, thus, to enable us to make our choices in a considered and deliberate manner. There is nothing in normative theory that enjoins either clarity of thought or error reduction. Just as we are required to check the internal consistency of an empirical theory, so are we obliged to check the logic of a normative theory.

More immediately, the great bulk of the value problems that arise in our classes, turn on the prescriptions and recommendations that we offer, the policies that we advance. These are propositions of an entirely different character and there is no reason why they cannot be treated as empirical claims. They must: for that is what they are. In my earlier reference to means-end chains, I indicated that the relationship between a means and an end is empirical. Policy preferences are intermediate between an existing state condition which is deemed undesirable and one that is valued. They are necessarily cast in the future tense and are of the classic if-then form: whether or not a particular policy will remedy the trouble it addresses, remains always to be seen. It is a fact, an assertion of fact, the validity of which has not been established.

Policies, thus, are to be treated as empirical claims—and the principle of accountability of assertion applies. If the range of application is specifically limited, we may take a policy as a hypothesis; if its range is wide, less empirically specific, we may treat it as a theory. Competing policies then are the equivalent of competing theories—and may, not so incidentally, serve to reduce error.

But this does not mean that policies cannot be or are not to be valued. On the contrary, they are assigned value precisely because they *prove* to be successful in producing the end-in-view that we desire. When, in fact, this occurs, we speak of a *good* policy; we may even *grade* it as the *best* solution to the problem we seek to eliminate. Were we to learn, once and for all, to treat the execution of a policy as an experiment, we would more easily learn what to value.

What of the ends-in-view, however, those on the far side of the chain—those that give direction to it? Friedrich once complained that such ends are rarely discussed in terms of their substance and he posed the following fundamental alternatives (ends): should economic development have priority; should it be agricultural or industrial; capitalist or socialist; should we give preference to democracy or bureaucracy—or, we can add, integrated structures vs. decentralized systems; ecological protection or maximum growth. The ends we can pose are legion. But each of these can also be viewed as a means.

For whether a preference is to be regarded as a means or an end depends on where it locates on the continuum. Our difficulties arise because we do not *know* which of these alternatives is best: which to value. Our knowledge does not reach that far; it does not permit us to grade accurately; to make the correct choice. If, in the future, such knowledge develops, as it has in many areas of our lives, we will be able to establish which of these alternatives is the most desirable with respect to further presupposed ends—which themselves will be generated by what we have learned. In the absence of such knowledge, empirical knowledge, we are obliged to, we have no other option than to cut the chain at this point and thereby establish ends. Thereafter, we argue over these on ideological grounds—often supported by faulty cost-benefit estimates, and we sustain our choices by showing them to be consistent with our prior values. It should be rather clear that over the length of a means-end chain, fact and value bear an inverse relationship to each other.

Finally, we need to take cognizance of the fact that our problems with respect to values have as much to do with their ambiguity as with their epistemological status. The term itself is not clear: its defining properties remain in dispute—a condition which also attaches to our primary normative concepts. But my point is not simply to suggest that our load will be lightened if we could reduce ambiguity; it is rather that ambiguity raises special problems in a scientific domain. Universally, such terms are frowned on; the overwhelming tendency is to expunge them from the corpus of a science. And the reason is clear: one cannot justify an equivocal assertion. I want to suggest, therefore, that the scientific resistance to including preferences in its claims is less a function of the status of the preference than it is of ambiguity. If ambiguity is eliminated, if value terms can be clarified, then—it is obvious, they can be employed. Applied science does so all the time.

V

I must now caution that if this paper constitutes a political act, if my effort is seen as "becoming political," then we have lost a precious stability of meaning.

FOOTNOTES

1. See William K. Frankena, "Value and Valuation" in *Encyclopedia of Philosophy*, Vol. 8 (New York: Macmillan, 1972 edition) for a convenient point of departure.

2. *Political Theory and Political Science* (New York: Macmillan, 1972).

3. I am sorry to say that he was correct.

4. This phrase is Henri Poincaré's. "Dangerous hypotheses" are those which are tacit and unconscious. "Since we make them without knowing it, we are powerless to abandon them."

CHAPTER 5

The Teaching of Political Science
as a Vocation

MARTIN DIAMOND
Northern Illinois University

Our subject is the relationship of the teacher of political science and the polity. More particularly, we are asked to consider whether "the teaching of political science is a political act." The very raising of such a question about this relationship—and the devotion of a conference to its consideration—presupposes that there is something problematical in it. To explicate that presupposition will launch us sensibly and sure-footedly into our subject.

On the one hand, common sense tells us that there is a tension, if not an ultimate contradiction, between the aims and needs of teaching political science and those of the polity. Education and the political strike even the untutored eye as belonging somehow to separate and perhaps even rival realms. That is, common sense knows that teaching has to do with the truth about the political, the truth wherever and whatever it is, while the political has to do with achieving or preserving what we here and now dearly hold true no matter what others may say or believe. But on the other hand, common sense also knows that teaching about the political is somehow also deeply involved with doing the political, that it is impossible to teach what is true about the political without thereby greatly influencing what people do politically. Common sense would appreciate, for example, that to teach as true what John Locke says about the origin and end of political society will tend to produce different citizens and statesmen than are produced by teaching as true what Karl Marx says.

This common sense awareness rightly sets the poles of our inquiry into the necessary but uneasy—in a word, problematic—relation-

A modified version of this chapter has appeared in *The Ethics of Teaching and Scientific Research*, published by Prometheus Books, Buffalo, N.Y., and is reprinted by permission.

ship of the teacher and the polity. Our task is to see more clearly, more scientifically, in what sense teaching political science both does and yet does not partake of the political character. We must understand about education and the polity what makes them separate and even rival realms and what at the same time draws them together toward a unity. If we understand this dual tendency properly, we may be able to find ways to conciliate the conflicting interests of education and the polity. Moreover, we may also thus learn how to teach with a rich relevance to the political the while preserving the detachment proper to the scientific. In any event, as the physician is rightly admonished to heal himself, so also are we obliged to make of ourselves and our enterprise a primary object of our political scrutiny. We cannot as political scientists ignore the political questions which the professing of politics itself raises.

I

Political science. Like all terms denoting studies of practice, how strange. The political is wholly bound up with *doing*, with the uncertainty and tumult and changefulness of things being made and done. The scientific is wholly bound up with *knowing*, with a movement toward the certainty, silence, and permanence of things being seen and grasped. The tension implicit in the subject of our conference—in the relationship of the teacher and the polity—is already foreshadowed in the very term, political science, by which we identify our profession. Science, as of course the root of the word reminds, means simply knowing. That is, however much the initial motive to the knowing, and the end to which it is directed, is eventual political action, political knowing tends to be complete within itself; like all knowing, it tends to culminate in a will-less seeing and in understanding truly. But the political is a will to action that never culminates and is a ceaseless shaping of events. We see this difference manifested in the very different kinds of human beings that politicians and professors become. We know that we professors, when true to our calling, are not the kinds of human beings who possess the political art, and that politicians, however wise and learned, are not professors of political science.

So great is the tension between the political and the scientific that Max Weber, for example, thought of them as belonging to wholly separate vocations or callings. This point he made dramatically in the two famous speeches he gave one year under the deliberately paired and polarized titles, "Politics as a Vocation" and "Science as a Vocation." This total dissevering of the political and the scientific is, of course, an expression of the like dissevering by Weber of value and fact. The political belongs for Weber to the world in which will passionately acts out "values," while the scientific belongs to a world in which fact is dispassionately studied and known for its own sake. Weber's fact-value distinguishing positivism led him thus to treat the political and the scientific as constituting unbridgeably separate worlds. But this is to see, and to absolutize, only the tension between those worlds which common sense understood; it is to neglect the contrary tendency, which common sense also appreciated, namely, toward the unity of knowing and doing the political. The title of this paper, a play upon the titles Weber used, points to the necessity of understanding the political and the scientific in both their separateness and in their unity, especially as that duality or tension confronts the *teacher* of political science. *Our* vocation holds both the political and the scientific together in such a way that the duality or tension, of their separateness and unity, is at the center of our enterprise. In our capacity as professors of political science, it goes without saying, we are not simply citizens or statesmen. But what needs saying is that neither are we simply scientists engaged in a silent, solitary study of politics. We are teachers of political science, and it is in our teaching that the duality or tension of the political and scientific comes into play.

Weber understood of course, that an academician unlike a solitary scientist, "must qualify not only as a scholar but also as a teacher."[1] Indeed he even calls this the "dual aspect" of the "academic process."[2] But by "dual aspect" Weber does not in the least refer to the political dimension of the teaching of political science; he means only that the academic scientist, in addition to his scientific qualifications, must also accidentally possess as a "personal gift" the pedagogic art.[3] Weber understands this pedagogic art very narrowly, as having no authoritative status of its own but as simply ancillary to the "scientific vocation." Teaching seems little more than a happy flair for presenting "scientific problems in such a manner that an untutored but receptive mind can understand them and . . . [most important] come to think about them independently."[4] Thus Weber gives only passing attention to the question of teaching and, moreover, he does so only under the rubric of the "scientific vocation." Hence the

very form under which he approached the question skewed his attention toward only what divides the scientific from the political and
away from what draws them together. But to repeat: We must understand that ours is not simply the scientific vocation, but a peculiar
hybrid vocation—the teaching of political science—in which the aims
of the scientific and the aims of the political are at once problematically
drawn both together and apart.

Not simply scientists, but hybrids who also partake of the political?
This sounds perhaps almost blasphemous to those who derive from
Weber. Perhaps it even sounds simply absurd. This is because Weberian
political scientists have a formal understanding of what is political
(and, for that matter, of what is scientific) that by definition makes
it absurd to think that the political could possibly intrude on the scientific and that, in the teaching of political science, some sort of peace
must be made between them. How the political is being understood
in this paper, therefore, had best be made clearer.

Weber understood the political in the following formulation:
" 'politics' for us means striving to share power or striving to influence
the distribution of power, either among states or among groups within a state."[5] In this tradition we have also Dahl: "A political system
is any persistent pattern of human relationships that involves, to a significant extent, power, rule, or authority."[6] If the political is thus understood, then the teaching of political science should indeed be utterly remote from the political, and it would be abominable and absurd to think otherwise. There should never be any "striving" in the
classroom "to influence the distribution of power . . . within the state."
In short, if the political is understood as thus narrowly confined to
the question of power, then the teaching of political science is most
emphatically not a "political act."[7]

Obviously, then, when I argue that the teaching of political science partakes of the political, I proceed from a different understanding
of what the political is. Easton's well-known definition moves in the
direction of the understanding employed here. In contrast with the
Weberian reduction to power considerations, which makes the question
of values simply epiphenomenal, Easton's formulation—the "authoritative allocation of values"[8]—tries to make a place closer to the center
for the "values" which are what the "authoritative allocation" is all
about. But the emphasis in Easton is inevitably still on the *process* of
allocation, which is power in a more sensible and genteel guise, but

power still. This is because, like all fact-value distinguishing political scientists, Easton has to treat values as subjective preferences deriving from objective underlying forces; and in the most important instances, this is ultimately to treat values as merely derivative of prior power distributions or relations. Easton's effort to restore the importance of value considerations in the political process was thus foredoomed. He was unable to treat seriously the most important political consideration—namely, what molds the values themselves? Where do they come from? Not only are they what political struggles are all about, but the substantive content of the "values" is itself perhaps the most important single determinant of what the "authoritative allocation" will be. This is simply to say that opinions about what is right and wrong are themselves the most important autonomous causal element in the political process. In short, we must understand politics as comprehending at least equally with power the purposes of power. And this means purposes, not as mere givens, but purposes understood as a people's ideas—their arguments and reasonings—about what sort of country they should be and the ideas of justice and human excellence they proclaim and live by or betray. Indeed, the way politics presents itself empirically to our senses is precisely in the form of arguments made by statesmen, governments, citizens, parties, and the like, regarding virtue or justice or the common good. Such rival opinions about what a country should do and what its common life should be are the politicsconstituting empirical stuff. What forms and influences such opinions, and what they influence in turn, is political in its essential quality. And we all know that such opinions—whether in the form of normative prescription or empirical description—are formidable causes of political behavior, indeed, the fulcra by means of which the levers of power work.

I suspect that every political scientist, no matter how narrowly he limits his formal definition of politics to the question of power, in fact proceeds in the classroom on the basis of the understanding of politics suggested here. To take a classroom example: We all surely treat seriously, in an American government course, as a political dimension of the presidency what Theodore Roosevelt meant in his fine phrase, "the bully pulpit." Indeed, most political scientists think a President fails in his political duties if he does not do well in his pulpit. (A value judgment, or a scientific statement about the nature of the presidency? But in any event, a teaching of students that molds their expectations of the presidency and to some degree, therefore, the kinds of candidates they will support.) Presidents speaking *ex cathedra*, as it were, powerfully affect public opinion on those underlying moral and philosophic principles, by the force of which "opinion ultimately governs the world." We professors of political science speak from a different chair—and the difference in the chair must constrain severely the manner and substance of our speaking—but ours too is a "bully pulpit," as we all know. Our teaching of political science inevitably speaks directly and closely to the purposes of power, to the "normative" issues of justice and human excellence, to "factual" questions of the nature and limits of the political. And by virtue of our inescapable impact upon opinion, our subject matter, unlike that of, say, geometry or logic, draws us inexorably into the political realm, both as it brings us to the interested attention of the political world and as we influence our charges in political directions. No formalistic definitional limitation of politics to manipulations of power will exorcize the reality: If we are in the business of professing politics, we are thereby in the business of influencing politics.

Perhaps at this point it will be illuminating, and prudent, to quote a great political philosopher whose good standing with modern political scientists is matched only by that of Machiavelli—namely, Hobbes. He says that, in defending their political interests, men switch from "custom" to "reason" and back again, depending on which at the moment supports and flatters them. That is why the claim of scientific reasoning, he tells us, in matters like "the causes, and original constitution of right, equity, and justice,"

> is perpetually disputed, both by the Pen and the Sword: Whereas the doctrine of Lines, and Figures, is not so; because men care not, in that subject what be truth, as a thing that crosses no man's ambition, profit, or lust.[9]

In our subject matter, the effort to teach the truth inevitably "crosses . . . man's ambition, profit, or lust." That is why, in a very special and constrained sense, and with inverted commas firmly in place, the teaching of political science may be considered a "political act."

But it is more accurate and less susceptible of mischief to say only that the classroom teaching of political science partakes of the character of political things. It remains now to explore that partaking by examining some ways in which the political and scientific are drawn together in the teaching enterprise, and how they are yet separate, and how this duality may be understood and lived with well.

II

An obvious and massive fact immediately differentiates the simply scientific enterprise from the teaching of political science: The teaching of political science, like all of education, requires that the teacher have students and money; it can't be done unaided and alone. And therewith the political by necessity intrudes upon the teaching of political science. In contrast, the scientific study of the political, in principle, can be conducted without the knowing consent of others, silently, alone, even covertly, and as cheaply as it takes the scientist to keep body and soul together.[10] The solitary scientist can live like a spy in the land, free behind his mask to behave solely in accordance with the ends and needs of his science. But when he becomes also a teacher of political science, he must come out into the open and accept the consequences. He must do whatever is *necessary* to secure students and money; he must do whatever is *just* with respect to these students and that money; and he must do the necessary and the just in ways *appropriate* to the ends of teaching so far as these differ from those of science or knowing.

As to the necessity: Someone always has to supply the books, real estate, food, wages, and the like—the necessary equipment. A lot of necessary equipment; Mark Hopkin's log would hardly suffice for our appetites and needs. But even more, someone always has to supply the young men and women who are to be educated. And the someone else, who pays and provides the young, always derives from or speaks for the ruling elements in the political order, whether it be parents, philanthropists, church, or the state. Now their money and their young are rightly precious to them and, ultimately, will be supplied only on terms, political terms. These terms vary with the varying needs of each polity and with the peculiar political and social demands each places upon education in general and the teaching of political science in particular. As it were, the constant—namely, the scientific study and teaching of universal truths about the political—has always to interact with the variable, the particular polity within which it must function. If teaching is to be possible—and there are times when it is not—some tribute simply must be paid to the dominant forces of each society. No accommodation to the political demands, no students and no money; no students and money, no teaching of political science. Sheer necessity compels teachers of political science to come to terms with the political element that is ineluctably part of their vocation.

For reasons both of prudence and science, therefore, political scientists are obliged to think through the best possible political terms for the teaching of political science. Prudentially, when one must come to terms with something, it is sensible to figure out in advance the best possible terms. But a scientific reason is likewise compelling. If accommodation to the political is necessary to teach political science, and if something like the teaching of political science is important in every developed society, then the terms upon which scientists teach politics are themselves a fundamental political phenomenon demanding to be studied. In short, the nature and history of that varying "interaction" between the scientific aims of the teacher and his constraining political environment is a subfield proper to political science. And the question that would have to guide study in the subfield can be readily stated. In studying how political scientists work out political terms in each society, the leading question would always have to be: Have the best possible terms been worked out here and, if not, why not? Whether the best possible had been achieved is the thing most worth knowing; moreover, only against knowledge of the best possible could one see and understand actual departures from it, rather like the way one has to understand disease as a departure from health.

With the question thus stated, the principle that would have to govern the answers immediately suggests itself. Namely: if political science *teaching* is to be worthy of the name, it must manage optimally in its peculiar circumstances not only to teach the young but also to preserve its scientific integrity; it must secure the best terms. And if political *science* is to be worthy of the name, it must state and defend the imperatives of science (which are "normative," be it noted) as valid and not as just resting upon some cognitively indefensible "value preference."

We may draw out the implications of this argument by considering it further in what is by now a familiar context, that is, in terms of the "political socialization" subfield so recently become prominent. The process whereby people learn and accept the political roles and values society assigns to them, we insist, is indispensable to the very existence of any society.[11] Well, then, how does our teaching of political science affect that admittedly indispensable political socialization? Does our instruction undermine what political socialization does? Should it? Will society indefinitely permit something indispensable to its existence to be undermined by those whom they pay and to whom they give their young? Should it? These questions would have occurred to Socrates; he would have seen the hemlock in them. But we have ignored them despite the fact that they must be asked on both prudential and scientific grounds. Scientifically, how can we ignore an important "input" into a vital political matter, especially when it is our own? Politically, how can we hybrid scientist-teachers fail to take the initiative and formulate those terms that will best accommodate the political and scientific interests which are entwined in our educational enterprise? This means to find the just principles and the rhetoric that will win for education, as we in our wisdom see its need, the public consent without which our enterprise is at an end. Securing public consent for the cause of knowledge by fair means: Does this not approach the essence of the political nobly understood? It is the political task our vocation imposes on us.

We have been able to ignore or blunt our awareness of this task which necessity imposes on us because we live in a country that defers to higher education, clumsily perhaps, but with an unprecedentedly lavish hand. This country has been not only generous financially beyond all our earlier expectations but also has been startlingly permissive in the intellectual latitude it has allowed to universities. But we must not be deceived into imprudent complacency or into scientific unawareness by the fact, for example, that Archie Bunker never brutally inquires into just what the "Meathead" is learning at that college. If only he knew. It is almost inevitable that some day he will and, then, the political constraints upon teaching political science will become dangerously clear.

But it is not only a matter of necessity or expediency that obliges the teacher of political science to come to some sort of terms with the polity. Justice likewise dictates such terms. If professors of political science are to take students and money, what are we to give in return? Justice requires that we return some sort of good to the students and the society, or perhaps a variety of goods according to the variety of students and the various aspects of society. And obviously we must at least be sure that we do as little harm as possible. Now for justice to be satisfied, we must be able to claim that the good we give is truly such. We may have a hard time convincing others; after all, it is in the nature of things that the highest education always has a hard time. But we must at least be able to convince ourselves that what we give is truly good and that others should also see it as such.

All professions and crafts—lawyers, doctors, carpenters—are under a like obligation; and I suspect most can make a better case than we have been making. Indeed, we have hardly even given serious thought to the problem of the consequences, as far as we can anticipate them, for sudents and society of our teaching of political science. It is not enough, for example, to have instruments to test the factual knowledge or general reasoning skills students do or do not acquire in our courses. Responsible teachers of a serious political science would search out deeper consequences of their actions, and then justify them or seek to avoid such as cannot be justified. For example, has the attachment of our students to their old pieties and loyalties been weakened in consequence of our teaching? Have they, as some think, been improved by that weakening? If so, precisely how? The customary justification for such weakening is that only by being emancipated from received opinions can students become "critically independent" in their views. No doubt. But is it only an old dogma among us that such critical independence is a good, or are we still able to make the philosophic argument to support our claim? For example, if all values are deemed equal from the point of view of scientific or cognitive reasoning, as is now widely believed, just how can it be claimed that critical independence is superior to uncritical dependence in the realm of ultimate values? (Indeed, in that realm of non-cognitive givens, what could the very words, critical and uncritical, independence and dependence, possibly mean?) It would be vulgar merely to assert that superiority as an article of faith; it requires a philosophical argument to sustain the idea of critical independence as the end and justification of our educational enterprise. Now that argument or justification originated in the Socratic tradition which modern political science has largely rejected. But having rejected the foundation, we blithely continue to assert the end; having rejected the argument, we still brandish the slogan. But if we are indeed to justify our impact upon our students, our weakening of their old pieties and loyalties, by the claim of "critical independence," then it becomes a compelling necessity that we restore our scientific entitlement to that justification. Yet who among us has even tried to face the issue openly, let alone think it through?

Further, do we succeed with all, most, or even many, of our students in achieving critical independence? Or do we leave most with their old beliefs disordered but without anything like the qualities of mind in their place which alone are the warrant for the disordering? Besides, is it really true that all we do is lead our students to think independently for themselves about politics? Is it not rather the case that the way most of us teach political science affects the views and characters of our students in a certain direction? If so, what is that direction, that is, what is the political bearing of the views and qualities that result in our students from our teaching of political science? Can we justify such a consequence? Further, do all acquire the same views and qualities or do these results differ among the different strata of our students? Are these strata not now extraordinarily varied due to our peculiar political situation, that is, to mass democratic higher education? Must we, and can we as scientists, take rhetorical pains to achieve the best results among all these strata? If so, how? Etc., etc.

The silent solitary scientist has no such problem with consequences because he only sees and grasps, but does not act upon and with others. But we do. And justice requires responsible inquiry into our own actions. We cannot take refuge in the position which may or may not shelter our colleagues in the physical sciences. We cannot say with them that we only teach the facts and that our students and society may do with them what they wish. Our enterprise differs from theirs. Nothing in what the physical scientist says about atoms and enzymes necessarily causes conviction in the minds of his students as to what should be done with the atoms and enzymes. But what we teach about politics does. The physical scientist teaches about matter external to the students; we teach them about themselves. As argued earlier, what we teach—whether descriptively about the nature, possibilities, and limits of the political, or "normatively" about the stands to be drawn therefrom—inescapably affects the most important political element, the fundamental opinions of our students as to how they and their society ought to live. No brandishing of an alleged distinction between facts and values, no positivist scruple will prevent our actions from having consequences, nor lessen the weight of our just responsibility for them. Moreover, not only justice but our political science itself requires no less: Can it be that we must scientifically inquire into every political variable except our own? No scientific scruple would prevent us from inquiring into all such matters as they derive from the behavior of the church, the military, the media, interest groups, and the like. Will we inquire scientifically into all politically relevant behavior save our own?

Now this just return incumbent on us as teachers of political science must conform to still one more constraint: The good we supply must be appropriate to our vocation, that is, a good given in our capacity as professors of political science, as sharers in an educational enterprise. That is how we solicit the money and the students, by promising the good that professors can give. If in our classes we try to be therapists, statesmen, or revolutionaries, we are, to say the least, taking money under false pretenses. That is a fraud, and not less culpably so for professors than for other humans. Now some among us may by gift or avocational development happen to be first-rate therapists or statesmen or revolutionaries. Fine. Let them be such in their private capacities and in their spare time, or let them fulfill their destinies elsewhere in the appropriate places. But we are talking here about the vocation of teaching political science. And there is nothing about professing which makes it likely as a rule that professors will be first-rate at anything else. There is nothing in the estate of teaching which supplies a moral or legal warrant for anything else than first-rate teaching. We have got to give only that good to our students and to society which we can claim to be peculiarly qualified and warranted to give, a good appropriate to the teaching of political science.

III

To this point, necessity, justice, and propriety, have emerged as standards for us, or constraints upon us, in our relationship with the polity. By emphasizing these political constraints, and by arguing that we must "come to terms" with them, I would seem to push us toward a mere subservience to the polity. I have had to stress this side of the problem because, in my judgment, the majority of political scientists, Weberians and also those who reject Weber from the "Left," have not rightly appreciated the inevitable and legitimate claims that derive from our relationship with the polity. In arguing that these claims cannot successfully, or justly, and not even scientifically, be ignored or rejected, I have of course stressed only one side of the dual tendency of the teaching-polity relationship, the side tending toward unity. But as indispensable as it is that we "come to terms," it is equally indispensable that these terms satisfy the other side of the tension that characterizes our vocation—namely, the side that has to do with scientific autonomy, with the search for political truth wherever it leads and without any deference at all to any particular policy.

One might say we are looking for some sort of mean. Not simply a compromise, an arithmetic mean which reconciles by merely splitting the difference, but a mean between the purely political and the purely scientific which is an "extreme of a kind," and which thereby enables the teaching of political science to achieve its fullest self, optimally satisfying both sides of its hybrid nature.

This sort of mean is usually found by considering dominant opinions regarding the matter under consideration. (Why that is a fact is itself a good subject for political inquiry; which is to say that the Socratic dialectic remains good political science.) Those dominant opinions usually fall into two strongly opposed groups. (Why *that* is a fact is another good political subject; likewise regarding Socratic dialectic.) In any event, in recent years there have been two such sharply opposed opinions or viewpoints regarding our subject—the "Weberian" and the view which opposes it from the "Left." By briefly testing each against the standards proposed—necessity, justice, and propriety—I hope the adequacy or inadequacy of each will become more evident. And I hope also that the mean we are seeking, and some positive suggestions for our teaching, will begin to emerge in the process.

Those from the "Left," who have in recent years rejected the predominant Weberianism of our profession, have challenged and shaken what might have become too thick a "cake of custom." They have made many valuable criticisms of the value presuppositions of positivistic political science. They have rightly sympathized with the yearning of at least some of our students for a political science that sheds light on their own moral and political concerns. They have rightly insisted that we cannot and should not seek to study institutions, structures, processes, power, behavior, or what have you, save as these bear upon questions of human value. They have rightly insisted that the study of politics is inseparable from questions regarding justice and the good life and the best political order. Had they stopped there or, more precisely, had they really dug in there and truly reopened the questions of justice and the good life, and developed both the "normative" and "empirical" implications of these questions, theirs would have been a powerful restoration of a profound political science.

But as far as I can tell, none of these critics of the "behavioral establishment" and of the "fact-value distinction" has taken seriously in the least the rich and ennobling perplexities of justice and the good life or of the "value question" in general. In all the prominent instances, or at least those with which I am familiar, they have simply dogmatically and passionately embraced one fundamental version of justice and the good life—namely, democracy understood only as equality, democracy made more and more democratic by equality being made more and more equal. They do not ask in the least that political science reopen the "value question," but rather in effect close it once and for all. There has not been a shred of questioning by them of their own ultimate values. They demand only that political science address itself to making democracy more democratic and equality more equal, and then stormily demand that the educational enterprise politicize itself to achieve the values they have embraced and in the way they have embraced them.

Consider the criticism these critics have made of pluralism in particular. The pluralists, they complain, have simply accepted as unchangeable reality the givens of present American political life and have, thereby, failed to see the possibilities for "creative" political action. And, they further claim, the scientific pluralist establishment has thereby provided an ideology, and made itself an apologist, for the American elite establishment. They demand instead a "critical" and hence "creative" political science. But the criticism, while generating some important questions and observations, is always and only from the "Left," and the creativity is always and only in the direction of the "Left." They have complained that American political science has been "closed," but theirs is an opening only to the "Left," which is at best to exchange one closure for another. We have instead really to "bust the case wide open." We have to reopen the value question and in prudent and appropriate fashion to follow it in our science and in our teaching as far as we can go.

Further, the issues raised by these critics of positivistic political science did not rest simply at the level of intellectual criticisms and questionings. There is also the problem of "politicization." These political scientists aggressively agreed that the teaching of political science is a "political act" in the most direct and grandiose sense, and they sought to make the campus and the professions centers of direct political action. But this is to ignore utterly the constraint of "necessity" upon us. The use of the classroom in pressing political causes will not indefinitely be tolerated by those who supply students and resources to the academy. The politicization of the classroom by the professor will result and should result in the politicization of the academy by the society. And an aroused society would never leave the academy in the quite free condition it now enjoys. Moreover, the politicization of the classroom by one professor would lead to a rival politicization by another, and so on, until the academy is made into a political community with majorities and minorities, tyrannies and factions, or into rival political communities, with conservative colleges, liberal colleges, and all kinds of political colleges. To some extent such divisions are inevitable and tolerable, and even, in small doses, healthy as a special brand of pluralism. But the degree of politicization recently sought, and the elevation of such politicization to high principle, would produce intolerable results.

It is interesting that many who call for the militant politicization of political science teaching themselves implicitly acknowledge the intolerable impropriety of such politicization, that is, as a regular principle for the academy. We may see this simply by paying attention to the common argument and rhetoric of the politicizers; namely, to the claim that we live in a moment of unique urgency. The argument usually runs that things are now so abominably and critically bad that every resource, including especially the academy, must be thrown into the struggle. But this is just a variation or subspecies of the old familiar argument that in a revolutionary crisis anything goes; that any human instrumentality may have to be perverted from its proper character and temporarily made to serve the revolution. This argument has, of course, nothing whatsoever to do with a principled view regarding the proper political duties or rights of the academy as such, but is purely and wholly a political decision. That this is so is testified to by the fact, which we all know, that such revolutionaries have no intention that political science teaching should continue to be a "political act" in their new just society; post-revolutionary regimes take great pains to assure that nobody like themselves will be in *their* universities. They know that permanent "politicization" is an untenable principle for education.

How may we sum up the viewpoint of these critics of Weberianism in terms of the standards that I have proposed? As to the necessity of "coming to terms" with the polity, they not only refuse terms but on the contrary insist that "critical" teaching *and* political action is the first duty of the teacher of political science. They take money and students from society and claim the right, both by teaching and by direct political action on campus, to rally the students and thus the society in whatever radically new human directions they conceive. Relatively safe because a sober majority of their colleagues provides a kind of shield for them, and because most western countries have been amazingly mild and permissive in their reaction, they seem to ignore the "counterrevolution" which their "revolution," if on a large enough scale, would inevitably, legitimately, and disastrously bring. Now this is all a judgment of fact and, regarding it, I think they are dangerously wrong.

As to the justice that the teaching of political science owes to the polity, far from ignoring the obligation, the Left critics of Weberianism make very great claims. They claim to give their students the immense good of heightening their moral sensitivity, summoning them to idealism, and helping them conceive politics in the light of a truly just political order. This *is* what a rich political science would give to all capable of receiving it, and here they would be very much on the right track: that is, if this meant teaching their students the subtle and poignant ambiguities of morality; if by idealism, they meant helping their students to become more virtuous, that is, more courageous, more moderate, more contemplative, etc.; and if they labored to open their students to the rival claims of variously conceived just orders. But instead they seem to have encouraged militant moral certainty; by idealism they seem to mean only the easy pleasure of railing at society while awaiting its moral transformation before achieving their own; and for them the just social order is not a profound and subtle idea to be understood and to be lived by as far as circumstances permit, but is rather an unquestioned goal passionately here and now to be grasped by the will and pursued at any cost.

As to the question of propriety, that is, as to what the teaching vocation requires and permits—what the teacher may fitly do in contrast to what the therapist, priest and rabbi, statesman or revolutionary may fitly do—no consideration seems to have been given at all.

*   *   *   *   *   *

We may reverse our procedure and begin by similarly summing up the Weberian position before we examine certain of its features in detail. Impeccable regarding the matter of propriety, Weber and his successors have said much that is true and valuable regarding the chastening constraints that the scientific student of politics must accept in his teaching station. They have said very much less about the problem of conforming to necessity, that is, the "coming to terms"; but there seems nonetheless to be an implicit Weberian strategy which we will consider. The fatal difficulty, in my judgment, arises regarding justice and the good which Weberians can claim to give to their students. It is in this respect that the defect of positivist political science for the teaching of political science may best be seen.

Little need be added here to the common understanding of the Weberian scrupulousness regarding what the scientific student of politics may properly do in the teaching position. Yet this much should be acknowledged: that scrupulousness has served the American academy well during the last decade. Scholars of the Weberian tradition, rallying in defense of the science which is their vocation, have ably defended the decorum and integrity of the academy and the learned professions.

We may turn immediately to the question of how Weberianism "comes to terms" with the polity. Since, as far as I can tell, it has said so little, we must search out its implicit strategy. This must be inferred from the functions or services or goods that Weberian political science claims to be able to perform. As we will see, these come down to two: clarifying values and showing how in the "real world" these clarified values may be maximized or optimized.

Now these services the Weberian offers to all comers alike. For example, Max Weber says that teachers should compare the various forms of democracy and then compare them with non-democratic forms so that "the student may find the point from which, in terms of *his ultimate values*, he can take a stand."[12] Any student; any ultimate values. The Weberian seems to believe that this neutrality will purchase freedom for his scholarly and educational enterprise. Not implausible. If you promise equal service to all, will not everyone be nice and leave you alone? Unfortunately, this works only in a liberal democracy. Only easy-going liberal democrats will allow Weberians to compare all kinds of regimes and let the student ultimately take his pick. Illiberal regimes—and not just modern totalitarian tyrannies, but respectable Puritan, Spartan, and medieval regimes, for example—would not allow any such freedom. The Weberian terms would be unacceptable to them and, on Weberian principles, political science could not be taught there. Is this not a fatal limitation? For if it is a fundamental fact about political life, as was argued above, that something like political science is and must everywhere be taught, then an approach to political science that limits its teaching to one epoch and to one kind of country is an approach that cannot account for a fundamental aspect of its own science.

Moreover, Weberian political science can only be taught in liberal democracies so long as it has no serious effect, that is, so long as the majority of students after such instruction come out relatively unimpaired from the point of view of the liberal polity. Remember that Weber commands the teacher to present to the student the various kinds of government so as to allow him to choose among them whichever he ultimately values. If we take Weber seriously, this means that, as a result of instruction in Weberian political science, many students might actually opt against liberal democracy. But if this really happened on a significant scale, the liberal democracy would soon have to clamp down on the subverting instruction, and then Weberian political science could not even be taught in a liberal democracy. And if it did not thus clamp down, the liberal democracy would soon be replaced by some illiberal system opted for by the now nondemocratic students, and once again Weberian political science could not be taught. The Weberian, then, is able to come to terms with the polity, but only a liberal polity and one in which he does not upset the applecart. This may do for a while and is sufficient for a parochial political science, but not for one that claims a universal scientific standing.

We must pursue a bit further this discussion of how Weberian political science fails to solve the problem of "coming to terms" with the polity, both to settle this matter and at the same time to form a bridge to our final question, namely, that of the good which the Weberian teacher of political science can claim justly to return to his students and to the polity.

Weberian political science, we must remember, necessarily "serves all comers"; that is, it presents its scientific findings in the same way to all students regardless of what their "ultimate values" are or become in the process. But this means to serve especially the ruling element in the polity, because that element is what typically prevails among the "comers." This is why Left critics have complained that Weberianism is a species of "establishment" political science. By abjuring scientific jurisdiction over "ultimate values," Weberian political science leaves these unchallenged; and that means to leave the prevailing ones, which is to say the status quo, unchallenged. But this is not the whole story. While it self-denyingly does not submit the prevalent and ruling "ultimate values" to scientific challenge, Weberian political science does not leave these values quite untouched. It undermines them—and all political values—by its radical distinction between fact and value and its denial of "cognitive" status to the realm of value.

In the real world, all "normative" theories typically claim to derive from reality and fact. Political scientists may postulate a radical distinction, but all "real world actors" believe and claim to derive their oughts from ises. They believe and claim to see in factual reality the pointers to the ways humans ought to live. Polities are in fact constituted by precisely such convictions; and holding such convictions in common is what makes them communities. Now Weberianism does not say that these convictions are false. It only says that science proves that no one can *know by reason* whether they are false or true "values."[13] But mild as this is, it is corrosive of political life which—and this, I think, is a fact—lives by the conviction that its beliefs *are* grounded in reason.

A simple example. American political life, we might all agree, rests upon (or at least once rested upon) the conviction that certain truths are self-evident. The Weberian necessarily answers: To you maybe, but not as such. No moral or political values, such as those in the Declaration, can have objective evidentiary foundation. Now most of us Weberians may, like you, happen to prefer to believe in the Declaration's "truths," but our science compels us to tell you that they are only "truths" to you and us, that is, for people with our "ultimate values." And they must, therefore, be treated by science merely as givens, varying from individual to individual, people to people, and age to age, but all incapable alike of cognitive foundation.[14]

But if it is a fact, indeed the premier political fact, that the vast majority of mankind believes its "ultimate values" to have such a foundation, and if polities are constituted by just such a belief, then, Weberian political science, far from *serving* all comers, is ultimately nihilistically destructive of all political values—at least, *as they are held in the "real world."*

With this, we have completed our discussion of the Weberian difficulty with the problem of "coming to terms," and have already begun to consider the just good which Weberianism claims to supply. To the student it says, bring to us your muddled values and we will help you clarify them. We will teach you to treasure consistency and thinking things through; we will help you to think your values through and to make them consistent one with another. But as to your deepest value, your "ultimate value," we say to you, do not try to think *it* through; it can't be done. Precisely when teachers should lead their ablest students to the deepest thoughts, Weberianism would seem to assure them at the outset that they need not make the effort. It assures them that they need not disturb their deepest prejudices, only their inconsistent ones. This is to assure the student scientifically that the world is a world of blind will, that his "value system" is a kind of weapon (or direction finder) that he must point while blindfolded, but with the guarantee of micrometric accuracy in every ancillary ballistic (or gyroscopic) detail. What sort of a "good" is that? And, in any case, why should one wish to perform it?

What of the second good promised by Weberian political science, namely helping the student to maximize or optimize in the real world, by means of scientific factual knowledge, his clarified values? The performance of this good would depend on whether the important (a value or a factual judgment?) real-world political facts would be accurately disclosed by a scrupulously value-abstracting political science. If it could be shown that important political facts are *thought* to be facts only on the basis of a *particular* value-orientation, then they would truly *be* facts only on the basis of the *true* value-orientation. If this could be shown, then Weberian political science, since it abjures the possibility of a true value-orientation, would likewise be incapable of truly disclosing factual reality.

There may seem something perverse in all of this to friends and fellow political scientists who are successors to Weber. I do not mean to be or appear so. Let me suggest briefly a way that will make my meaning clearer and less perverse-seeming. The difficulty may lie in the word *value*. It is only two centuries ago, as far as I can tell (which means largely by recourse to the Oxford English Dictionary), that the word came to be used in contradistinction to *fact*. This revealingly modern usage has a rhetorical effect. It almost requires that one think of facts as radically separated from values: First one sees the facts and *then*, separately, one values (or likes) them or not. That is why I have sometimes used the word *value* in this paper with a kind of demurral indicated by inverted commas. I do not accept that the question is whether I like or value the facts, but rather it is a question of the inherently "valuative" nature of important political facts. Compare the case of medicine. We do not ask a doctor: a) is that a cancer? and b) do you like it? We ask him: Is that healthy or diseased tissue, no matter whether you happen to like (or value) it or dislike it? We know that he cannot see the fact of cancerous tissue save on the basis of a true understanding of the distinction of health and disease, no matter which he prefers or values. What I am concerned with as a political scientist is very much more like health and disease than valuing or liking.

Some of the difficulty can be traced, perhaps, to the way the English language translates as *virtue* the ancient Greek *arete*. For us, virtue came to mean morality which became moral *preference* which became *liking* or *valuing*. But *arete*, I am told, meant something much more like health, or better still, excellence. Thus Plato and Aristotle spoke about the health or excellence of the body as *arete*, and then also, using the same word, of the political excellences and the excellences of the heart and mind. They did not understand how the body could have its health or excellences, discoverable by appropriate scientific inquiry, and the heart and mind not have theirs, discoverable similarly, albeit with much more difficulty and perhaps uncertainty.

It seems inescapable to speak of a fact-*value* distinction—facts separately first, values separately later. But must one, can one, likewise speak of fact-*health/excellence* distinction—facts separately first, health/excellence separately later? What I am suggesting, less perversely it will now appear, I hope, is that political facts and political health or excellence are not radically disjoined; and that, indeed, important facts *are* such only in the light of a true grasp of what is healthy or excellent political tissue. This is the crucial issue. If one accepts what I have suggested, then the question of whether one should *value* healthy rather than diseased political tissue would not prove very troubling.

I suggest further that the only worthy political science is one that undogmatically, without any pretense to having the answers, rediscovers the perennial questions about political health and excellence, and takes its best reasoned shot at them, always aware how easy it is to err in such matters, and therefore always awaiting the discovery of its own errors so that it may improve its questioning and answering.

Not to proceed in this way, but rather to teach our students that there is no "cognitive" basis for questions and answers about political health and excellence, is to make them scientifically armed philistines, armed by us with a scientific defense against all the pain and beauty of truly political, which is to say human, inquiry.

IV

It is always easier to show what are the defects and excesses to be avoided than positively to state what the mean is. But that does not lessen its existential reality or lessen our access to it; as it were, although it may not be painted in bold colors, it is still there and visible in the central area not shaded in on either side. Still we must try to make some positive suggestions.

As to necessity and the "coming to terms": if the polity is truly abominable, then open higher education in political science is impossible; teachers and students will be able to proceed only covertly if at all. After all, the good man can no more be a good professor of political science than a good citizen in a truly bad regime. There is not sufficient political health or decency in such a regime to supply a common ground for teacher, student, and the society. But in any decent regime, and I affirm emphatically that ours is, a political science oriented to the question of political health and excellence will be able to come to teaching terms.

The way to come to respectable terms is to give to the decent polity and its constitutive opinions a central and respected place in the teaching of political science.[15] One should begin by considering what the decent polity regards as its own excellence. This would mean in America to begin with the founding documents of this political order, the Declaration of Independence and the Constitution, and to teach the student to see as deeply as possible what are the claims of his own regime, what it regards as the proper human ends and the modes of their political attainment, and what is distinctive in all this as compared with political behavior elsewhere. And it would mean to study, by the light of those ends and putative modes of attainment, American political institutions, processes, events, behaviors, in all their manifestations.

To make this the starting point and the rhetorical mode whereby the student commences the study of politics is the way to secure the best possible terms for the teaching of political science. The decent polity is thereby assured from the outset that, whatever may be intrinsically dangerous in teaching the young about politics, the danger has been minimized by a prudent political science. Such a political science will win for itself the greatest possible latitude in pursuing its autonomous scientific ends. Moreover, this is not only a prudent concession to necessity, but it is also in principle the dialectically sound way to begin the educational ascent. The cleverish dialectical procedure is to take delight in showing what is wrong in a proposed opinion; the Socratic procedure, as in the opening discussion with Cephalus in the *Republic*, is to begin pleasantly with what is sensible and healthy in the proposed opinion. By this means, a student is led affirmatively through his received political opinions toward the full explication of what he believes. To explicate fully means to develop precisely the meaning, nuances, grounds, and implications of these opinions. When that affirmative explication of the opinions is completed, their problematic aspects will soberly have been disclosed. One will have begun with the familiar and will step by step have rendered it problematic. By this time the deeper and universal questions, the questions which transcend any particular polity and which are the universal stuff of an autonomous political science, will fully and yet safely have been raised. The full explication of received decent opinions culminates in philosophic understanding. Thus what begins as a prudent concession to necessity and as a basis for "coming to terms" with the polity satisfies also the autonomous needs of political science. What I suggest, then, is that to search out what is politically healthy in one's own regime (which is ultimately also to consider what is not healthy in it) is the path to the mean we are seeking, the mean that will satisfy the dual needs of our hybrid vocation, namely, both the tension and the unity in our relation to the polity.

This same mean meets also the test of *propriety*, that is, our obligation to function only in a manner conformable to the teaching vocation. What could be more faithful to that vocation than the effort to instruct each in accordance with capacity, abjuring as far as one can all political means of coercion and persuasion, raising especially every consideration, as Weber somewhere says, "that tells against one's own position," holding nothing back ultimately, and drawing—educing—from each student as best one can what is excellent in each relative to the study of politics? By freeing ourselves from the self-denying ordinance of the fact-value distinction, and turning instead to the question of what in fact is healthy and diseased in political life, we are enabled to find our proper posture, namely, neither unconstrained scientist nor committed politician, but instead the mediating teacher between the two.

Finally, as to *justice* and the good we must give in return: The recommendation I have made for the supportive but ultimately philosophic consideration of the decent polity, in our case, of the American liberal democracy, has the great advantage of avoiding the harm we may inadvertently give. When millions go to colleges and universities, some are unfortunately not capable of it. As it were, the many and the few are now to be found in each classroom. Political science, it must be remembered, is strong stuff; it can injure those incapable of handling its demands. Every teacher has had the experience (although not all know it) of unintentionally injuring some of his students. Some shatter religious beliefs, others debunk sexual "mores," and others mock the "values of the marketplace." Still others incautiously or too loudly teach philosophic truths that cannot be received with understanding and prudence by young students.

The danger is not only that individual students can be left disoriented, less decent, less capable of common sense; but the danger is on a large enough scale now that the regime may be deprived of the kinds of citizens it needs. This danger is averted, I believe, if the sympathetic consideration of the American regime is properly stressed in the teaching of politics. When this is done, each student will be more likely to take from his education what he is capable of receiving. Those students who can "go all the way" will have been given sound guidance; and those who inevitably "drop out" along the way will have had their opinions and characters improved by what they were able to understand. Please note: nothing is held back from anyone. It is all there, democratically available, in the books and in the discussion. None are let in while others are barred; no special decisions have to be made. But the presentation is structured so that the desiring and able and the persevering simply select themselves.

Still further on the good we ought to give. There is something more even than a just return for the money we take and the students we receive. It is a good we seek for ourselves and can delight in sharing as teachers. It is fitting that I illustrate this with a quotation from Leo Strauss, whose teaching, many will recognize, is the source of what I have said here to an extent greater than I can justly acknowledge. It is a quotation from a lecture he gave in class at the University of Chicago shortly after the death of Winston Churchill.

> The death of Churchill reminds us of the limitations of our craft, and therewith of our duty. We have no higher duty, and no more pressing duty, than to remind ourselves and our students, of political greatness, human greatness, of the peaks of human excellence. For we are supposed to train ourselves and others in seeing things as they are, and this means above all in seeing their greatness and their misery, their excellence and their vileness, their nobility and their baseness, and therefore never to mistake mediocrity, however brilliant, for true greatness. In our age this duty demands of us in the first place that we liberate ourselves from the supposition that value statements cannot be factual statements.

Let us only "liberate ourselves" from that supposition. Let us only *reopen the question*, the perennial question of political health and human excellence. We will then avoid the *defect* of either making science sterile or, more likely, of having unphilosophically to smuggle our values in, thereby deceiving others or, worse, ourselves. And we will at the same time avoid the *excess* of taking our values as settled, and needing only our passionate commitment to them. If only we "liberate ourselves," we may then find the mean and with it be back in our proper business: raising the perennial questions, offering the evidence against our answers as well as the evidence that inclines us to them, and sharing prudently with our students the love of asking and seeking.

FOOTNOTES

1. *From Max Weber: Essays in Sociology,* eds. H. H. Gerth and C. Wright Mills (New York: Oxford University Press, 1946), p. 133.

2. *Ibid.,* p. 130.

3. *Ibid.,* p. 134.

4. *Idem.* Although it exceeds the purposes of the present paper to pursue the matter thoroughly, we must at least note what Weber's view of teaching capacity as an accidental personal gift implies. So accidental is it, in his view, that he regards it as "a matter of absolute chance" whether scientific and teaching capacities are found together in the same person. Now if this coincidence is a matter of "absolute" chance, then there must be absolutely nothing in the nature of pedagogic capacity that makes likely its possessor also having a scientific capacity, and, likewise, absolutely nothing in the nature of scientific capacity that makes likely its possessor having also a pedagogic capacity. But his view flouts commonsense and reality. Granting the utmost to idiosyncratic and accidental qualities of good teaching like vigor of speech and manner, erotic disposition, patience, the like, does there not remain in the scientific capacity and understanding itself some crucial requisites of teaching? Whatever might be the case in other disciplines, it seems impossible for the scientific understander of politics, precisely in virtue of his science, not to be also the best understander of how to present the subject to "an untutored but receptive mind." Or such at least would have been the view of all pre-Weberian modes of political analysis. For example, Platonic, Thomist, Lockean, and Rousseauan political science would have held scientific and teaching capacity naturally and largely, not accidentally, to coincide. What then is it about Weber's science that causes him to see the radical disjunction? This question leads us back, of course, to Weber's positivistic distinction of knowledge of value from knowledge of fact, and his excision of the former from the purview of science. But since in the nature of things, education and the question of values are inexcisably linked, Weber is led to divorce absolutely teaching capacity from scientific capacity. For such a political science, teaching apparently can only be understood as, say, a species of charisma, a mysterious, accidental, purely personal gift. But perhaps that is one of the things wrong with such a political science.

5. *Ibid.,* p. 78.

6. Robert A. Dahl, *Modern Political Analysis* (2nd ed. Englewood Cliffs, N.J.: Prentice Hall, 1970), p. 6.

7. It should be noticed that Dahl, like many American political scientists, while following Weber in confining the political to the question of power distribution, departs from Weber in an important respect: Dahl omits the qualification Weber made, namely, power relative to the *state.* Now this may be insufficient; Weber may have been too formalistic in this qualification. But it at least saves him, it seems to me, from a difficulty into which Dahl is betrayed by his broader definition. Consider the curious fact that, on Dahl's broader definition of the political, the classroom would seem to be an arena *par excellence* for political acts. There is in the classroom, in my own at least, a very persistent pattern of human relationships that involves authority to a very significant extent indeed. As in deciding what we study, what we read, who speaks when,

what testing is required, who gets what grades, etc. Now this kind of authority, on Dahl's definition, would seem to make my classroom a thoroughly political place. But *classroom* authority, in my view, has nothing to do with *political* authority; it is a kind of authority that derives its warrant from the scientific and educational side of what goes on in the classroom. Defining the political as power distribution or as rule or as authority perhaps begs the question. The question remains: What *kind* of power, rule, or authority, is *political?*

8. David Easton, *The Political System* (New York: A. A. Knopf, 1953), p. 129.

9. *Leviathan,* I, 11.

10. Cheaply, unless you happen to need survey data, computers, research assistants, travel grants, interviews, access to governmental data, etc. Come to think of it, political science thus conceived not only cannot be studied cheaply, but can only be studied in a certain kind of liberal democracy; which would seem to mean that such a political science, while preening itself on its unprecedented universality and detachment, would in fact wear the blinders resulting from its limitation to liberal democratic data. Talk about a relationship of political science to the polity. This would be a case of symbiosis.

11. Political socialization, strange term that. We let sociology a long time ago abscond with the "social," and now we timidly seek a small share back, by claiming that the political is an important subset of the comprehensive set, the social. Perhaps we ought to reclaim our entire estate, by more assertively, and yet justly, naming this subfield, *social politicization.* This would be the process whereby the immature are, by merely social means—because that is as yet all they are capable of—prepared for the mature roles and values which the political community requires of them. This change in terminology would reflect an old recognition that the political is not merely one of many aspects of society, but rather that political opinions and practices architectonically give to the whole society its distinctive character.

12. *Op. cit.,* p. 145. Emphasis supplied.

13. See Arnold Brecht, *Political Theory* (Princeton, N.J.: Princeton University Press, 1967), pp. 9-10, 124-26.

14. *Cf.* Leo Strauss, *Natural Right and History* (Chicago: University of Chicago Press, 1953), pp. 1-2.

15. I have drawn here from an earlier paper where I dealt with this matter at greater length and in a different context. See "On the Study of Politics in a Liberal Education," *The College,* December 1971, published at St. John's College, Annapolis, Maryland.

CHAPTER 6

Political Science and the Undergraduate

ALLAN BLOOM
University of Toronto

I

Reflection on the training of undergraduates is not only an obligation imposed on us by our functions as teachers, it is a salutary opportunity for us as scientists and scholars to reassess ourselves and our discipline at a time when it is directionless and in disarray as well as having lost its appeal to students. The younger student—not yet committed to any profession, still open to various temptations and blandishments, in need of inspiration, learning and guidance—provides an excellent focal point, for in thinking of him we are constrained to think about what we should contribute to the formation of a whole man and what we actually are contributing to that formation. We must try to determine where political science fits in the scheme of the sciences and what role its study plays in the economy of the soul.

This kind of return to our origins has been sadly neglected. For a long while a combination of self-satisfaction and the hopes generated by the new scientific project in politics kept political scientists from serious reflection on their pedagogical responsibilities, except to the extent they sought for recruits to the new science. Being unattractive to undergraduates became almost a hallmark of the seriousness of a political scientist—showing that he had divorced himself from vulgar common sense and youthful enthusiasm, that he had become like the physical scientist in his laboratory. Then, when real politics made insistent demands, some political scientists returned to the young, not as teachers but as followers and demagogues, and extorted promises from the other political scientists in their newly donned white smocks that what was going to emerge from the laboratories would be of benefit to the activists. All this was only response to immediate pressure, not serious re-thinking. Political science curricula are now un-

117

structured heaps, reflecting unarticulated tastes and compromises reached for the sake of domestic tranquility. They reflect no agreement about what political science is or what kind of training makes a political scientist.

To put it bluntly, students and citizens in general have an instinctive awareness of what politics is, but political science does not have any view of what it is, or at least not one that in any way corresponds to or refines that untutored awareness. This makes political science repulsive or at least uninspiring to students. It is no accident that the student political movements of the sixties had no roots in political science, were uninformed by real political knowledge, were in part directed against social science, and found among political scientists only a few late supporters who were afraid to miss the wave of the future. They were neither inspired by political scientists, nor restrained by them, nor educated by them. Their intellectual sources were in sociology, philosophy, and above all literature. Political scientists had not anticipated the movement and had nothing to say about it.

Now the awareness of which I speak is that politics has to do with justice and the realization of the good life. Somehow the authoritative political decisions about war and peace, who shall govern, education, etc., appear to determine our way of life. Politics is the arena where we most effectively settle our destinies, where we fulfill ourselves and the best of us win glory. As such it makes the highest demands on our bodies and our souls; it can at least make a claim to be the natural end of man. The quest for community in political practice and values in political theory which animated radical students was an expression, however distorted, of this political awareness and need. Aristotle was not enunciating a personal doctrine but merely giving voice to the citizen's perspective when he said that the *polis* is the association whose end is the highest and most comprehensive good, the one that includes all other goods and on which they depend. The citizen has perhaps been frustrated by modern civil society as a whole, but he has most certainly been frustrated by political science from which he had a right to expect instruction and clarification about the ends of politics and the means available to him for fulfilling them. He has been largely left with his inchoate sentiments, either quiescent or raging.

To survey the difficulty one need only look at contemporary

political science and compare it with the political science sketched by Aristotle. He called it, corresponding to its subject matter, the architectonic or master science, the one that ordered all the others, the queen of the sciences, the one that treated of the highest good, the enlightener of citizen and statesman. Our political science would not impress anyone with an imperial claim; it is one of the least reputable and advanced of the modern social sciences. It is the oldest of the social sciences, with a history going back to Socrates, whereas most of the others are of very recent origin, and all were founded in conformity with the project of the new natural sciences of which mathematics was the queen and back to which all the others were to be led. While the older queen was deposed, she has proved to be an intractable subject, resisting reduction to more primary sciences, her matter intransigently demanding common sense in order to come to light, qualitative distinctions in order to maintain its proportions, judgment about good and bad in order to be intelligible. Economics could, by abstraction from political reality, find quantifiable units, but the economy remains only a part of the political order, subject to and requiring the guidance of politics, the cause of great distortions if emancipated. In the first place, then, political science needs both a basis for a common good and an irreducibly political dimension of human nature, but it cannot find them any more and is at least partially committed not to finding them.

Further, political science is a halfway science in another way. It is both practical and theoretical. Political science is intended to assist the statesman and the citizen. It is also in quest of an understanding of human nature. These two functions are at a certain tension with one another. Theoretical impartiality is easily compromised by political commitment, and practical usefulness is frequently despised by the new scientists. And practice is in its turn corrupted by abstractness and doctrinarianism. Actually, however, the two sides contribute to one another—the perspective of political actions providing the subject matter and the concern, the perspective of theory providing the distance and reflectiveness which can both correct policy and give us the opportunity to escape the limits of our own time and place. But the new political science has eschewed this productive tension without fulfilling the demands of one side of it or the other. The "serious" political scientists tend to despise the practical perspective as journalistic or worse. But their science does not attain to the level of an explanation of political man. A famous political scientist once asserted to me that it was wrong for the APSA to invite famous political figures to address its conventions. "They are our data," he said. "When physicists have Geiger counters giving speeches at their conventions, then I will think it right to let President Truman speak to us." I doubt whether a political science which looks at statesmen and their concerns as a biologist looks at genes through a microscope is even possible. It would certainly be irrelevant to an undergraduate student who is going to be a voter or who hopes to be a politician. One of the most salient characteristics of many political scientists is that they are not interested in politics. Aristotle considered political science to be but a refinement of such an interest; new political scientists pride themselves on a radical break with it.

There is a final reason for political science's problems with undergraduate education, and this one is only in part due to the behavioral movement. Political science is no longer able to distinguish between the important and the unimportant, the central and the peripheral. Aside from the methodological considerations which helped to blur these distinctions, the simple growth of the sub-disciplines in the last twenty years has covered over the core to such an extent that one wonders whether it is there any more. The expansion of the universities, their willingness to respond to ephemeral demands, and the encouragement of foundations brought a horde of specialists—particularly in area studies—into political science departments the studies of whose fields should have been relegated to research institutes but who as professors had to teach courses and who constituted a voting majority in matters of department policy. Now, for example, it is difficult to find courses taught in Western European politics and difficult to find teachers for them, while areas of secondary significance for the understanding of politics are overrepresented. I would venture to suggest that American politics, international relations, and political theory are what every student most needs to know about. I do not think the required instruction reflects this, to the extent that there is a required course of instruction.

What political science education ought to be can be inferred from what I am saying it is not. It should concern itself with the great political issues—freedom, equality, virtue, religion, family and patriotism. It should provide an experience of political action and principle as well as providing a model of a reasonable approach to these issues. It should appeal to the student's heart while calling forth his reason. It should at least make a case for the integrity of the political phenomena. It should concentrate on method only to the extent that method contributes to the elaboration of the questions of primary concern. It should show the various possible regimes and the arguments for and against them—particularly in the intention of avoiding the cloying cycle of conformism encouraged by contentless, unprogrammatic rebellion.

II

It is obvious that the incoherence of undergraduate education is a result of behavioralism, its attack on traditional political science, and the various responses to behavioralism. And the resolution of the problem would require a fundamental transformation of the profession's current self-understanding, for the undergraduate training will inevitably reflect the most respectable views held at the highest levels of the discipline; everyone looks to the top, and in the major universities the teachers are the same as the scholars. There is not likely to be both a political education and a political science education when the demands of the two are so disparate as they now are. Thus, although what I suggest is simple, in the current situation it is utopian. However, a few further remarks are appropriate. They may be of use to individuals or small groups of teachers who are interested in politics and suggest a stategy for their educational endeavors.

In the first place, there is no doubt as to what is attracting the students at all levels: political theory. In the major universities where theory was not abandoned, the theory offerings are the most popular, and graduate applicants list their intended specialization as theory more than any other. In the others there is a persistent clamor for the hiring of theorists. There are a lot of bad reasons for this renaissance of theory. On the surface, it seems to be the easiest thing to study and to provide the maximum opportunity for self-indulgence, gab, and indignation. In some quarters theory has meant little more than a cynical and self-serving outlet for anti-establishment sentiments and has become a grab-bag for every trendy movement of letting go and irrationalism. The taste for political philosophy can have its source in this generation's peculiar combination of intellectual laziness and desire for authority. But this taste gives evidence of a healthy instinct which, it trained, can bear serious fruit. That instinct is connected with the desire for living a good life, the further desire for enlightenment about what a good life might be, a longing for alternatives to what is available, the sense that the excitement and morality of life are to be found in politics. Underlying the behavioral movement in the U.S. was the conviction that all questions of principle had been solved by the advent of the New Deal and its ultimate universal acceptance and that what remained were questions of appropriate means. The current generation has taken cognizance of the shattering of that conviction, the end of the end of ideology. The study of the great texts in political philosophy attracts and sublimates this primary instinct, and by way of them the student can be led toward the careful study of concrete political reality. It is from the discussion of the good life and the just regime—and the demonstration that the books of tradition are the basis of this discussion—that one must begin with this rootless and largely unpolitical generation.

At this point I should pause to make two comments on the character of undergraduate students today, apart from the orientation toward jobs of which they are too frequently accused. (1) They do not have that everyday interest in politics as it is practiced which an older generation had. Who's in? Who's out? is not the substance of their daily consciousness and conversation. They do not follow events and personalities, either domestic or foreign. They are very private, and political events impinge on them only in fits and starts, usually in an ideological way and without detailed knowledge. Thus they do not have the stuff out of which political reflection is made. (2) This is not a reading generation. They do not enjoy reading. They read because they have to for classes or for information. There are almost no fundamental books which form their souls, which provide a common core of learning or a viewpoint. There is nothing like what the Bible, or Shakespeare, or Locke or Marx or Freud meant to earlier generations.

Both of these factors provide an obstacle to political science training. Students must first become involved in books. The books must be presented to them by teachers who care about them, know them, believe that they contain alternatives which might be chosen by their students, and can communicate some enthusiasm for them. A good example of a book well suited for this task is Tocqueville's *Democracy in America*. At first sight it appears a bore to the students—long, outdated, and descriptive of what they think they already know. But when they become aware, for example, that Tocqueville in describing the democratic mind describes their mind and that that mind is gravely limited in its capacity for the sciences and the arts, they begin to take notice. Tocqueville argues that contained in the very principle of democracy is a tendency to intellectual mediocrity and conformism. This is a troubling assertion, one which the student is likely to discount for his own protection and because he has almost no experience of intellectual greatness. Coordinate with the assertion about the intellectual mediocrity of democratic man is the assertion that aristocrats are likely to be superior in this respect. Now aristocracy is something about which the students know nothing except for certain tales and which they simply identify with oligarchy. They are forced to look to another regime, one which denies the fundamental principle of justice—equality—which all accept and to which they are devoted. They find there are arguments on both sides of the issue, and they take democracy more seriously in calling it into question. They start looking to the practice of democracy, to historical examples of other kinds of regime and above all to the best arguments for each—none of which is simply contained in Tocqueville but to which he points. They are driven out of the narrow confines of the impoverished contemporary alternatives, but they also look at the present more closely. Is there a tyranny of the majority? What can a "power elite" be in a democracy? And Tocqueville also warns that egalitarianism can lead as well to despotism as to freedom. The study of modern tyrannies takes on a new meaning in this light. Tocqueville both teaches about the broadest themes of politics—and does so with a precision based upon experience and observation—and is also himself a model of a political scientist.

In the context of such studies, which would broaden out to the entire history of political philosophy, a student would surely want to know about voting studies; but they would be subordinate to considerations of the issues in elections, and they would surely be less important than the study of the *Federalist*. Statesmanship will be a more fundamental study than statistics. The students must get involved with the great political figures, try to determine what constitutes their gifts, whether they can really influence affairs, what the relation of their prudence is to morality and justice.

Once enthused and politicized they must study history and do detailed analyses of other regimes that have accomplished great things, some past, others contemporary—the peculiar genius of British parliamentary government and its imperial achievements, that of the Roman republic, etc. Particularly useful is Soviet politics because there Americans, who can hardly really imagine another way of life as essentially different, can immerse themselves in the horrors of a modern tyranny. What is needed is not scientifically neutral studies of development or of managerial elites, but description and analysis of how this regime affects the lives of its subjects, what its goals were, how its rulers found a way to govern so securely. I do not mean that this study is unscientific, partisan, or undertaken with a propagandistic intention. It should be a dispassionate observation, but one that stays close to the questions that any thoughtful man would ask in deciding whether he wants to live in a regime. The student should be open enough to recognize that current American standards are not the only grounds of judgment, but no one's sensibilities should be so dulled by false science as not to recognize murderous despotism. A decent political science must know what everyone knows, that Watergate is bad, and its horizon must also be broad enough to make it impossible to mention it in the same breath with—not to speak of assimilating it to—the Gulag Archipelago. It is here that the fact-value debate becomes frivolous. Regimes such as that of Stalin or Caligula cannot be seen for what they are if one has been forbidden to think of them as bad. It is too simple-minded to say that we must study facts, then teach values. The facts contain the values; the separation destroys both. The study of these foreign regimes should not lead to self-congratulation and is not intended to contribute to any political movement. Its purpose is to understand the nature of political things. When the name of Hitler can be invoked to qualify Richard Daley, political science has failed in its most elemental responsibility. It is our duty to teach about such things. A generation of graduates has been produced from our universities who do not have the slightest idea what Fascism was. Neither the important facts nor the principles of judgment have been learned.

Along with political theory, the sub-discipline which has attracted and stimulated healthy political interest is international relations. Because war and peace are of such immediate and intense concern, even to political scientists, politics among nations has defied reduction. Most of its practitioners talk about real situations and not abstract models. The enormous stakes involved in political life are most clearly felt here, particularly so today when the confrontations involve differences of fundamental principle as well as oppositions of will. Therefore a truly political judgment is maintained so long as the issues are matters of life and death. Policy orientation helps keep the focus which we are too likely to lose. It risks degenerating into journalism or preoccupation with daily affairs; it can also easily involve the temptations of being too immediately useful to power, actual or anticipated. But one can learn a lot even from those who are so involved. And if the temptations are properly controlled, the international stage is one on which the broadest spectrum of political motives can be played. All the aspects of the statesman's art are revealed there. The relation between the predictable and the unpredictable, nature and chance, become serious questions and can be concretely posed. The relation between justice and survival, principle and expediency, come best to light. The necessity and the difficulty of judging between conflicting claims become manifest. Most of all, the harsh side of life and the real problem of combining humaneness with success can be shown to young people without experience of necessity and imbued with great hopes. Living through the problems of foreign affairs is a good education in the nobility and baseness of political life and helps the student to liberate himself from the doctrinairisms of principle and method. At best it can lead him to contemplate the alternatives contained in the somber gentleness of Thucydides, the hopeful brutality of Machiavelli, and the strict moralism of Kant.

I am not arguing that a similar movement from the practice of politics to the primary theoretical issues could not be made on the basis of American politics. But given he current state of the discipline it is much harder to do so. Aron and Kissinger are closer to politics and to philosophy than are Dahl and Easton.

III

A proper training in political science must not only address itself to the student conceived universally but also to the contemporary American student, by which I mean it must correct the characteristic intellectual defects of our regime. Every regime tends to develop certain potentials at the expense of others, and a good education attempts to counterpoise this tendency for the sake of the intellectual freedom of the individual and in the hope of mitigating the excesses of the regime. Here again Tocqueville is a good guide. The central weaknesses of egalitarian Americans to which he points and which political science training could help to rectify are the following: (1) a privacy which focuses on petty concerns such that the individual finally cannot lift himself to great issues; (2) a lack of grand ambition; (3) a lack of respect for tradition which ultimately impoverishes their understandings due to a lack of awareness of alternatives; (4) an addiction to abstract ideas; and (5) a readiness to accept deterministic explanations of things, resulting from a sense of the individual's weakness and tending to re-enforce that sense of weakness. All of these inclinations have become more pronounced since Tocqueville's time, and social science is both an expression of them and a further cause of them. With respect to weaknesses (1) and (2) above, social science has concentrated on unpolitical and ignoble motives for everything and particularly political action. With respect to (3), social science method both implicitly and explicitly denies the truth value of older books, and its peculiar brand of empiricism has confined it to recent, and particularly American, experience. With respect to (4) and (5), social science wishes to establish general laws like those of the natural sciences, ignoring the particularity of which politics is largely constituted, and those laws would leave no room for the rational choice of citizen or statesman.

The political science for which I argue and which is really at hand would act as an antidote to these moral and intellectual vices. (1) It begins by taking the political on its own terms and giving it and the motives connected with it a substantial and irreducible existence. (2) It provides a ground and a goal for the peculiarly political desire to be first, to be honored and win glory. It also provides examples and objects of admiration. (3) It makes it possible to see the wisdom in old books and the questions they raised. Our horizons are broadened by the presence of real alternatives to them. Instead of our scrutinizing everything else, we are scrutinized by the great thinkers of the past. (4) Although looking for general rules, it contains no doctrinaire assurance that they are to be found, and is open to the possibility of choice and accident. Moreover it pays particular attention to the concrete and the heterogeneous. (5) It stays on the level of the phenomena and does not explain away the manifest examples of political choice, undetermined by circumstance, affecting the most fundamental political things. It is, thus, an education in freedom and human dignity without intending to be so.

In my experience the student caught up by the newly discovered possibility of rational reflection on justice and happiness also rediscovers the lost idea of the university—the university, today so much maligned and so uninspiring. He begins to read history for examples. He finds that the greatest literature has a political intention and gives the perfect representation of the essential political-moral problems and the heroes who grapple with them. He begins to see the importance of rhetoric for the persuasion of men. He finds he must look at science, both to evaluate its proper role in society and to find what it teaches about nature in general and hence about human nature. He finds the lost key to the unity of the sciences and thereby to a liberal education. Nothing fancy or particularly new is needed—just teachers, students, books, and a calm setting in which rational discourse is respected. By contemplating politics and its limits we face again the questions without which no life is human: freedom, virtue, god, love, and death.

CHAPTER 7

Becoming Political

HENRY KARIEL
University of Hawaii

His sententiousness notwithstanding, Hegel surely had it right: when exits close and options are cancelled our vision is suddenly sharpened and we can catch ourselves in the act of seeing. An auspicious moment for educators. Now that few people suppose the future will be better or that, in the end, we will finally have arrived somewhere, it has become less embarrassing to see ourselves where we are, to comprehend progressively more of the present, to make more of ourselves.

*

They don't teach you suffering at Yale, Charles Newman told an English socialist. They teach you to hate the people who don't hate it.

*

In art and education, though, nothing whatever is necessary: we are free to do otherwise. We are free from necessity and can refrain from loving and hating, from going all the way, from ending. We need not come out anywhere. If, then, still in search of some definitive self and community, we should not establish much of consequence—as we are beginning to anticipate—we can nevertheless remain in possession of the process of establishing nothing much. An endlessly redeeming possession, the process itself can provide the ground that allows us to keep moving. The process itself, once looked at, may be seen to constitute the educational enterprise. Being in control of it we can cut into it and hold its possibilities in words. By speaking up, we can let others know about its etiquette, obligations, rituals, and rewards. And as we come to express its inherent promise, we may be struck by the way it resembles not only artistic processes but also political ones: basically it is all about performing, acting, and

This essay has previously appeared in *Teaching Political Science*, Vol. 4, No. 1, October, 1976 © Sage Publications, Inc., and is reproduced by special permission.

participating in public arenas, a presentation of self, a showing and telling, an ongoing demonstration, a continuous effort to disprove the notion that those in power are authorized to rule and teach.

*

"The value of opinions" (in its context, Max Frisch's epigram sounds less assertive) "is in direct proportion to the share of future time remaining to the person holding them." Our opinions as teachers have diminished in worth, and it is surely time, or at least no longer untimely, for all our conclusions to follow. Opinions, findings, results, conclusions—the stuff of texts, dead weight.

*

I think we could bear the loss of our conclusions once we saw that we would be left not with nothing but the *process* of losing—itself a discussable and publishable enterprise of many dimensions, the stuff of community and politics, the political process in concentrated form. Were we to realize this it would matter less what, specifically, we choose to express in the classroom, in lectures and publications, in encounters with students and colleagues. Seeking no effects, our performances—provided they are structured so as to call attention to themselves—will naturally exemplify aspects of politics. Showing ourselves in action, we will ineluctably provide a model of the process of politics. We will be getting and keeping the attention of a welter of scattered interests—engaging in politics—no matter how specialized our concerns because, in any case, we relate not only whatever might be our own preoccupation but also whatever expresses everyone's need to communicate. *To the extent that we succeed in calling attention to the process of communicating itself, making it explicit while holding the attention of others, we will enable everyone to gain political knowledge.* Even our most specialized activities will then demonstrate that political life has no definitive end, offers nothing of consequence, constitutes no more than the ongoing process of communicating, and becomes visible quite beyond all specific goods and evils as our only public treasure.

*

"Well," she said, "if you are communicating that, then you're not communicating nothing, are you?"

*

Any course that goes beyond its proclaimed subject matter to reveal its constitution will, to that extent, turn out to be a course in political science. If this remains largely unacknowledged—and if we would like it to appear less strange—what can we *do* to implement it? How, in practice, might politics be taught more explicitly? That is, how can students generally be enabled to experience that politics, like the educational process, is an altogether inconsequential, ambiguous, open-ended, genuinely playful enterprise? How, despite our various preoccupations, despite our determination to get somewhere and say something, can the interminable educational process itself become the explicit subject matter of what is called teaching?

We could do worse than Henry Adams who, after knowing he had nothing to teach his students and was but educating himself at their cost, decided, as he said, to hold his tongue, and quit Harvard College. We can follow Adams because he kept using words to *say* he would be silent, because he kept offering more advanced courses. We, too, can provide time and space, make room in which to resist the profundities of the day, and avoid conclusions. We can offer way-stations, asylums, retreats, stopping points, interregna, and moratoria, incomplete courses, fragmentary essays, fragile models—in short, endless opportunities for interminable learning.

*

"Please consider me a candidate," I wrote on the grant application form. "I am very much concerned with designing a curriculum that would do justice to the contingency, openness, fragility, and fragmentariness of our experience by noting how these qualities are reflected in the formulations of contemporary literature, science, movies, etc. What we currently seek to transmit through schools, mass media, and universities is knowledge of completed acts rather than of the processes that lead to and beyond them. We stress art objects, scientific formulae, laws and decisions, true meanings, and correct explanations rather than people in the process of performing, creating, playing, politicking, participating, and simply *acting*. I would wish to have us turn toward processes and away from completed (or abandoned) works, deeds, and achievements. This shift—which our educational enterprises should capture—has been perceived by Daniel Bell, Hannah Arendt, and Irving Howe (with regrets), by Harold Rosenberg and Robert Jay Lifton (with a measure of ambivalence), and by Ihab Hassan, John Cage, and Richard Poirier (with enthusiasm).

I would hope to clarify and legitimate the ground for this shift in orientation."

*

It is not all that hard to imagine the appropriate course and to envisage students signing up because they wish to learn about political processes and about methods for ordering and sustaining them. All who enroll (let us pretend, simulating assurance) really want to be introduced to progressively more of politics as well as to progressively more of political science. At different levels of complexity, they all seek to enlarge the range of their comprehended experience—specifically that part of life that has been labelled "political" insofar as its "power" is "organized" and its "constituents" are "governed," insofar as its "scarce resources" are variously "allocated." With the help of a strange terminology—alien words such as paradigm, charisma, legitimacy, equilibrium, and that final catch-all, political culture—they may find it possible to perceive and establish unfamiliar aspects of their experience. All members of the class are (as my image has it) in action, attracted or pressured to mediate among conflicting interests and to block overbearing ones. The situation is wholly political. All of them, it would seem, are in the business of staging performances.

Such action, I realize, constitutes the hidden curriculum of *every* course. But while every course of study serves to make previously unacknowledged interests appear in some public space, political science courses deal with political concerns quite explicitly. I know this preoccupation with politics may not be much in evidence. Understandably, past experiences have made everyone reluctant to express interests by participating in the process of learning: most of human energy is devoted to perfecting strategies of withdrawal. We should therefore not expect that those who have agreed to take the course (or to offer it) are likely to risk displaying themselves as participants, as individuals interested in taking and playing parts. To act, we know, is to be suspect. The actor betrays our repressed indifference to endresults. He reveals a lack of commitment, an exasperating avoidance of climax and consummation, an intolerable rejection of utilitarian calculations, a lamentable hostility to achievement, a shocking conviction that each of our moments is sufficient. No wonder that prospective participants who admit to their need to perform and participate express this need initially only in the minimal act of filling out a registration form or, in the case of instructors, of letting some departmental committee know of their interest in teaching the course. Given such diffidence, few in the course will display more than their barest inclination to participate more fully.

In my postulated setting, however, their incipient interest is likely to become increasingly manifest. Because *no* end results are promised, because all conclusions are postponed, students and instructors alike will finally desire to *do* something—anything—just to make the time pass. They will desire not merely to serve time but to give some meaning to it. Occasionally this political impulse may remain so repressed and distorted as to seem absent. Or it may find appreciation and expression in other courses, in off-campus activities, in family life. As a consequence, apathy may well be manifest both among students and instructors.

Assume, however, we can risk waiting. Surely some members of the class, at least the one who had offered to instruct it, will be aware of the satisfaction that comes from self-expression. They will know how gratifying it can be to move beyond the silent, inert, dismal reality which is manifest. They will begin to use words and gestures and visual aids to *make* the class meaningful. Getting pleasure out of communicating (also being paid or credited for it), these activists will disclose themselves *doing* things—claiming the floor, asking for time, and, of course, mainly talking. They will use found objects, given materials, innocent questions, or made-up structures as points of departure. Presumably, they will do the best they can: remembering and recalling, quoting and paraphrasing, sharing propositions, perspectives, and insights, inviting objections which promise to advance their discourse. To attract and hold everyone's interest (their own as well), to avoid, as I said, serving the time they have been allocated, they will have to express themselves in whatever ways prove to be attractive— that is, *interesting*. And they will thereby be *doing* political science.

*

In giving expression to dramatic experiences and in employing interest-holding modes of comprehending themselves in interaction, some members of the class—officially titled instructors—will of course be more knowledgeable than others. Perhaps because they know themselves to be closer to the end of their lives, they will seek to appropriate each moment more fully, more able to recall and offer what they know. Yet equality reigns: whoever can draw on his knowledge to engage others will have emerged for that time as de facto instructor. Whoever will have signed up for the course—one designed to introduce students to political processes—will in effect engage in activities of his own making and employing the discipline that enables him to comprehend and take pleasure in his activities.

I would suppose we may still feel guilty because we suspect conventional material will never find its way into a course so empty of predesigned content. We might expect everyone somehow to perform without providing advance scripts—but will it be political science? Yet I think we can relax about this if we remember that even when left free to wallow in spontaneity we nonetheless tend to be so constrained that it would seem safe enough to do anything imaginable. The liberal imagination is not so exotic and rich that it will threaten the status quo. Within our society encounter groups are apt to become as routinized as free schools. Before we know it, content emerges. What we have been conditioned to define as facts, problems, and functions shapes up so quickly that what we actually do turns out to be fairly conventional stuff. Giving expression to whatever dismays or pleases us, and taking pleasure in calling attention to the modes for comprehending ourselves in action, we have good cause to expect political science's ordinary subject matter and conventional concepts to emerge. Ogg & Ray remain as alive as Burns & Peltason. The world as known is all too fully with us. Instead of worrying about the absence of overaccredited substance, I think we might be gratified that our course might allow for a gain in form—a self-reflective form within which we can both experience politics and *get to know ourselves in the process of experiencing it.*

*

Donna Zucker said it first in a letter: to get more politics into our essays and our living spaces, we must move by indirection. "We employ a language that is oblique, vague, abstract, indirect. And suddenly, we have something, possess something, see something that goes beyond mundane experience, that creates the possibility of, indeed defines, a new reality."

*

It was a set-up. The week before, I had performed in Wayne Fielder's section of the introductory course. Introduced by him at that time as guest lecturer, I related how I had come to change my mind about some of my previous judgments. Students asked various questions after I inquired if everyone present could really agree with *everything* I said.

Reappearing now, I need no introduction—and by prearrangement with Wayne, get none. He seats himself on one of the two chairs at the side of the classroom next to Elly Edmunds, a fellow teaching assistant who has stopped by for the occasion. I move myself behind the desk in front, sit down, and lean slightly forward, looking expectant. I display a readiness to wait, to take my turn. In our society, a feminine posture. I seek to appear not indifferent but as *determined* to say nothing. A slight smile from me—and a few smiles from several students. An air of anticipation. Silence slowly stretched beyond convention. I lean forward a bit more as if to say "Well?" Slight embarrassment everywhere. Faces turn to the side, eyes shielded. It is not that nothing is happening but that I, in the seat of authority, am earnestly trying to make things happen.

Wayne glances at Elly. He smiles conspiratorially. Out of the heavy silence comes a rasping cough, covered by another cough from the other side of the room, as if echoed. The first cough is repeated. I think of two drummers in the jungle, realizing I must have missed previous smaller gestures, an array of far less audible efforts to communicate. Someone moves his chair, scraping it along the floor. Failing to remain uncommunicative, I now move mine a bit backwards. One student opens a newspaper at the very moment that another starts to read the book she has in front of her.

Only four minutes have elapsed.

Wayne whispers to Elly and she nods in agreement. Two boys begin to talk to one another in whispers. The girl who had started to read writes a note and passes it to her neighbor. I am dying to know what it says and don't mind looking curious. The note is passed on, read by another girl, and returned with a knowing smile. Smiles suddenly light up this entire group. Several communities have emerged during my mute presence. Wayne and Elly. Two coughers. Chair movers. Two boys. A group of three note readers. At least five groups have transcended reticence and made their appearance.

On my right, an older student now grins broadly, his eyes very open. I grin back at him. "I guess," he starts slowly, "you're wondering what sort of questions we have after the last time." I look at him encouragingly. He continues: "You said something about the way. . . ."

He goes on and reviews what he thinks I said, ending with a question about it. Everyone is wholly attentive, focusing on me. I find it oppressive to say nothing, to offer no relief. The same student comes to our aid: "I guess when you said that, you must have meant. . . ." And he explains what he thinks I must have meant, looking at me, begging for confirmation. At this point, I am ready to confirm anything, but there is no need because another student proceeds to exclude me by referring to me in the third person: "He didn't mean that at all. What he really meant. . . ."

A total of eleven minutes had passed, and a miracle had occurred: two people actually began a discussion and others listened. In a setting in which the alternative to communication was some form of isolation—boredom or withdrawal or self-absorption—people had begun to relate. It is not much of a discussion—but it is theirs.

It only remains now to keep it from seeming miraculous, to reveal its normalcy, to make quite explicit that its emergence was no accident at all. Accordingly, I now break in fully, as I had planned, and summarize what I think I saw and heard. I end by asking others to give their account of what had transpired. It is easy now for everyone to act as a political scientist, to take note of the conditions under which communities might be formed: of who leads and who follows; of the role of founding fathers; of the relationship between sex, authority, age, and participation; of the segregation of late-comers; of the prerequisites for development; of the very foundation of politics. Holding the mirror up to the class, I am aware of the infinity of possibilities.

There is talk of this meeting for months.

*   *   *

"My job," Robert Altman was quoted as saying in *Newsweek*, March 11, 1974, "is not to create a work of art but to reflect on the process of it."

*

The strategies for extending the resonating silence of a particular class are familiar even though their relevance to classroom situations remains unacknowledged. Insofar as artistic modes of action conform to a discipline that frees us to keep moving, they constitute a model on which I should like to elaborate, hoping we will simultaneously see it as a model for becoming political. Works of art can be seen as displaying how specific conclusions are jeopardized when placed in wider contexts, how inarticulate private feelings are identified when expressed in public places, how seemingly inexpressible pains and pleasures are redeemed by politics. Artistic works show the *uses* of devices such as pauses, interruptions, redundancies, reversals, transpositions, ironies, repetitions, indiscretions, digressions, inversions, juxtapositions, exaggerations, conceits, and deceptions—all contrivances for shifting one's loyalties from the successful to the defeated, from the soothing surface facts of life to the uncouth, wild interior, all devices invented to bring *order* to one's passions. They find concentrated expression in a posture defended by Robert Frost whom another poet, Peter Davison, quotes in *Half Remembered* (1973):

> Shiftiness. It's a good word. Shifty. You gotta shift back and forth between loyalties. . . . You got to shift a little here and shift a little there to get along. But you gotta get a long. Gotta shift. We say makeshift. Shifty. Nothing wrong with that. We gotta make shift.

The continuous shifting of focus and inflection enables us to alienate ourselves from mindless experiences, from the dead weight of prevailing definitions, reifications, and finalities. We are directed to undercut the ends of our current experiences, by depriving each of our propositions of the conclusiveness inherent in our lives, in our very grammar.

When we keep our assertions ambiguous, when we decline to say clearly what factors make a situation "critical," we make it possible to see that a crisis or problem for one group is a solution for another —and that the only *un*critical condition is the unimaginable one that includes the claims of all. To accept this posture is to be skeptical toward every prevailing structure and function—except, of course, our own skeptical disposition.

*

Responding to the general human need to remove blocks to self-expression, the artist subscribes to a discipline that enables him to doubt whatever he (and we along with him) have been driven to experience as real beyond doubt. Furthermore, his reality-enlarging process is so organized that he (and we as well) are led to abandon whatever structure he designed so as to make him (and us) more fully active. His discipline disrupts routines and multiplies relationships. It complicates the presumed exigencies of life and logic. Generating tensions, it keeps us at tension. While the artist's work makes us alive to new ventures, it de-eroticizes our old investments. It de-reifies whatever objectives we have embraced with singular intensity—whether money, sex, status, pleasure, or power. Just as these objectives threaten to claim our *full* attention, works of art redistribute our feelings about them, detaching us, for example, from genital sex or established power centers and attaching us to unappreciated zones of our existence. The artist, it should be clear, redeploys interests by creating arenas within which our focus is changed. Thus Richard Schechner, founder of New York City's Performance Group, has converted "found space"—streets, mountainsides, warehouses, meadows (though no classrooms) —into theatrical space, using it to heighten the experience of actors and spectators, enabling them through deliberately designed rituals to reach a higher state of self-awareness. He made each performance a *rite de passage* through which all participants are to be transformed. On entering the theater to see "Dionysius in 69," each spectator is separated from whomever he accompanies so that he must make a separate entry. For "Commune," the audience must surrender its shoes when entering. For "Makbeth," it moves through a maze before climbing down into the playing area. Everyone involved is a protagonist. Everyone must choose how extensively to participate, going through some agony, seeing his stable conventions tested by alternatives. As director, the artist creates opportunities for encounters, wounds sensibilities, slaps at coherence, opens space where none had been suspected. He instructs everyone—including himself—to court misfortune, to let go of familiar pains and pleasures so that it becomes possible to master more of both. He adds modifiers to beliefs we had come to regard as settled. His distinct discipline consists of systematically undercutting what he appears to assert, scrupulously displacing and reversing himself, destroying well-known plots and sequences, implying the opposite of what he affirms. He leads himself and others to see the teacher as student, the doctor as patient, the hero as villain, the fool as sage. He shows wardens to be their own prisoners and the rich to lead impoverished lives. He shows good causes—like evil ones— to have another side. Whether assertive or seductive, his work gives indubitable villains and heroes their moments of doubt.

    The artist enables us to realize that reality is neither objectively settled nor "given"—not even by him. Leaving traces of his own pres-

ence, letting on that his vision is distinctively his, he implies it is *merely*
his and that others might proceed differently and establish different
realities. Leaving the frame vague and the center ambiguous, he implies that not even his expressions settle the boundary and meaning of
a situation, that others might draw new boundaries and create new
meanings. By including irritants which detach us from his work, he
moves us to encompass and appropriate more of reality, to enlarge
the setting of known experience, of our own cramped lives. His work
acts first to attract us by indicating (in documentary fashion) that
something really is "out there" and then to alienate us by refusing
to place things out there definitively that we might believe him and
let him have the last word.

   All decision-making processes may in fact be seen to embody what
is distinctive of the artist's mode of action. Legislative processes that
demand the recognition of interests other than the legislator's own,
methods of inquiry that force us to confront counterarguments, or
courses of study that elicit commitments to conflicting points of view
—all these are expressions of a discipline that demands testing some
private interest in a public setting. Although these processes are os-
tensibly concerned with outcomes—a law, a scientific proposition, an
educated individual—*the results are present every instant*, and they
continuously give the pleasures that inhere in performing and politicking, testing and probing, acting and playing. Being neither circum-
scribed entities nor finished achievements, such processes suspend the
distinction between means and ends while disabusing us of the elite-
serving notion that gratification comes only at the end, that everything preceding the end is but a burdensome preparation from which
it's best to spare the mass of people. An artist's work may therefore
be seen not as some end-product but rather as the very ground on
which everyone (the artist included) can keep from ending.

   To maintain this ground the artist will confront the present state
of things—himself included—but not accept it as complete, as having
ended. He will ask questions not likely to have been previously asked.
How would people behave under changed conditions? How would
they perform on different stages? If resources not currently available—money, love, status—were provided, how would his characters
respond? What potentialities would be realized? What new dimensions
would come into play?

   In such interrogations, the artist treats the present as ambiguous and proceeds to contradict it. Violating what is so clearly the case, his symbols put what we know to the test and thereby serve to exhibit unknown possibilities, hidden capabilities for action. Works of art—whether novels or communities of living men—are thus experiments: they put existing worlds into crucibles and transform them under controlled pressure.

At its most powerful—in the forms advocated by Marx, Dewey, and Sartre—overt action replaces vicarious experiences: it presents concrete alternatives, constituting visible displays of previously unacknowledged options, public demonstrations of the practical feasibility of continuous social development. Such action is exemplified by public performers as diverse as Mailer, Malraux, Duchamp, Russell, Muhammad Ali, Godard, and Mishima. All actors, they include parts of themselves in their field of operation, communicating both what they do and what transpires in their minds. They show themselves opening up, taking things in, changing in the process of observing. In each instance, as they exhibit themselves, they become the spokesmen of unexhibited elements in the lives of others. They represent suppressed realms of being. And just as their acts threaten to become unbearable—just before we shudder and break out in embarrassed laughter or tears—they enable us to *see*. They make more of life accessible to us by inducing us to acknowledge that the world, viewed comprehensively, is both the best and the worst of all possible ones. Their transactions not only expose the refractory givenness of our existence, the dense and authoritative inevitability of the way we happen to be, but also vindicate our freedom to put all remaining authority to the test. Treating what lies beyond inexorable necessity as open—as *not* necessary—they are committed to the proposition that the truth lies only in the unrevealed, ineffable, incommunicable whole. They thereby imply that *our* truths are only so-called truths, mere surfaces and fragments.

And what of the actor's message, *his* truth? It is trustworthy only because not offered as such, because it is advanced in the form of disclaimers, proclaiming itself to be other than what it seems. Its author —to say it ponderously—knows that he knows not. We can trust him because he manifestly does not trust any specific aspect of himself: whenever he concludes, he treats his conclusion lightly. He removes mysteries and taboos by not caring too deeply, by not pursuing truth too intensively, by pretending to let truth come—and dismissing it in his very effort to share it. In different terms, he treats himself negligently and, like model teachers or psychoanalysts, will ask to be discharged as expendable. To succeed in this educational role, he allows himself to be recognized as forever taking the other side. Merely *appearing* as truthful, he lets on he is a prevaricator, *Doppelgänger*, impersonator. His very conduct denies the reality that meets our eye.

Works of art, *all* appearances, will ideally *train* us, as Morse Peckham has noted, to stand our ground even when we are losing our footing. Inherently inconclusive, designed to maintain suspense, they prepare us to withstand the continuous pressure to become a partisan of but one side, to make up our minds, to arrive at conclusions. By participating in the artist's project, we learn to endure situations in which nothing seems to fit, in which everything seems deranged and unfinished. His work reduces the violence, exploitation, and cruelty in our midst simply because it opposes forces that make us apathetic. It extends contexts, making specific situations less flat, monotonous, inane, stale, simple, banal, dull, and familiar. It moves us away from sensory deprivation and loneliness—all blocked eroticisms.

It is precisely within the open spaces in which art is practiced that we can keep relearning to recognize the evil of conditions devoid of context—the quintessential quality of pornography. Space articulated by art reveals the obscenity of all forces of final consequence, all those conclusive triumphs that deflate the ego and put us to rest. The resonant space that art creates discloses the presence of immanent, realizable alternatives. It lets us realize that there is no *need* to be satisfied by the way things are, that so-called reality can be made to cry out for change.

Whenever we transform external and internal reality, we express our artistic impulse, our basic need to change desolate, disgusting, sickening, and finally deadly forces—evil situations—into life-giving ones. It is not that creative activity converts brute elements in nature and in man into objects of beauty but rather that our very action—not its end-product—prevents us from becoming brutalized, from becoming dead objects. The artistic process itself—the treatment of everything seemingly completed as subject to reconstruction, reinterpretation, and review—humanizes us, enhancing our powers. It enables us to develop unfamiliar aspects of ourselves as well as to cope with the dehumanizing aspects of new conditions, of new varieties of evil, exploitation, violence, brutality, and meanness.

Artistic processes—play, experiment, ongoing testing of self and others—are thus the very conditions of human survival. Making us conscious of usable, self-sustaining resources within ourselves, they induce us to disrupt overpowering routines. Time and space for play and art and politics consequently enable us to adapt, to prevail, to become what we are.

*

Thomas McGuane has the hero of *Ninety-Two in the Shade* (1973) observe that if you look life straight in the eye, it will kill you: "The great trick, contrary to the consensus of philosophy, is to avoid looking it straight in the eye. Everything askance and it all shines on."

*

If a class is no less a work of art than any structure deliberately designed to enable us, as Frost said, "to get along," it too can be seen as a political arena, a boundary-breaking enterprise, its objective not prefigured, its participants not inclined to "cover a field of study" during some set hour, week, or semester, its material not knowable before its participants find themselves moving through it. It follows that the character of a class, like the character of a playful exercise, can be *known* only after it has run its course and become exhausted. What the exercise is really all about can be known only to the extent that knowledge is jointly defined in a process which, on the most abstract level, may be seen as interchangeably artistic and political, a process involving all who have enrolled, all who are loyal to nothing save the most comprehensive point of view attainable, all who remain committed to an unfinished, ever-expanding context for specific experiences.

*

Were we to move ourselves through political science on these premises we would come to see that participation in deciding on appropriate subject matter gives opportunities for calling attention to the process of deciding—and therefore to the nature of politics. We would no less realize the need to express our distrust of predefined problem areas and established content, of textbooks and lectures which presume to an air of reality.

There is a loss in this that may be hard to bear for those now in authority. After all, they are asked to welcome a transfer of trust to whatever groping figures might join courses in political science. To

what extent can we *all* tolerate the loss of confidence in the very notion of hierarchy and authority? To what extent can we support instructors who fail (as we still say) to structure courses prior to the
first day of class?

Perhaps we can find some comfort in noting how possible it actually is to keep hedging and shifting and equivocating, to keep seeking derangement, to *appear* professorial without *being* professorial. Is
it not possible to remain quite carefully split, to let neither side win
over the other? At that decisive place where "two roads diverged in
a wood" (as Frost wrote in "The Road Not Taken") we would have
to be able to take the high road as well as the one Frost made famous
even though he never settled for it—"the one less traveled by."

While I seem to be taking the high road—I am *responsibly* dis-
coursing—I have in fact gradually stopped evaluating, ranking, and
grading in relation to authoritative standards. Further, my courses,
seminars, meetings, and publications have become increasingly choppy,
fragments of an unknown whole. The line between my class and my
home has begun to fade; private matters emerge in class and public ones
at home. My projects fail to begin in the beginning or end at the end.
Earning "incompletes," I enlist others even before room assignments
have been made and after deadlines (curious word) for grades have
been passed. I announce no expectations save one—that I have none.
I don't prepare students or myself for Bigger Things to Come. I offer
no background, conduct no survey. I expect no one to have satisfied
prerequisites for enrolling in my courses and specify no criteria others
must satisfy for teaching, for being promoted, or for becoming tenured.
I no longer wish to wait until sixty-five before disciplining myself to
treat the times and spaces which lie ahead as potential spheres for
play and politics.

While on occasion I still feel the need to pretend to uphold standards, I have ceased to insist on conforming to them. Pretending to
be free from the dictates of reified authority, I move myself toward
forms of action grounded, it seems, in nothing except everyone's need
to exhibit more aspects of himself in plain view of others. I know
of no limits except those set on the one hand by the terror of boredom,
the deadening effect of dull repetition, and on the other hand by
impending embarrassment due to more self-exposure than we can tolerate without trembling. Either of these puts an end to the educational process—to politics—and both therefore define my limits.

When I feel enervated and can't find support in forms as insubstantial as suggested by this elaborate hyperbole of myself in action, when I reveal my weakness by being garrulous, defensive, strident, or sentimental about my new-won discipline, I experience a crisis of sorts. Guilt breaks in. There is surface anger and subsurface panic. "Should I really stop grading?" "Should I vote for tenure when no one can tell if he is really worthy of it?" "What is the real constituency for my published reflections?" "Who is really listening to me?" Students feel no less anxious: "What am I really getting out of this course?" "Why should I really work when the instructor keeps saying I should only do what I want to do?" Frenzy, dizziness, paralysis.

But I think it is possible to cope, to manage even after withdrawing from the opiate of authority as we quest for the really real. Though whirling, we can recurrently see that we actually have assumed responsibility for ourselves, gained in independence, and proceeded to govern our own conflicting impulses. And occasionally we can profit from unexpected support.

I have found a measure of legitimation for my posture in one of Richard Schechner's performances of "Commune." In August 1972 in Vancouver, he invited students to come early when the cast was assembling at six:

> About ten students showed up [as Schechner tells it in *Environmental Theater* (1973)], and they entered the theater together with the performers. The visitors were to go wherever they pleased. They watched warmups, listened to notes, helped the technical director check the lights, set the props, fill the tub, clear up the theater. They watched the performers put on their costumes and saw the regular audience arrive at 7:45. Then the performance. After, the routine of closing up the theater for the night: removing costumes and putting them in the laundry bag for washing, recollecting props. . . . The performers were a little uneasy at their presence for warmups and notes. After the performance no one minded who was there. I felt funny, too, and performed a little for the "real-time" audience. . . . Removing the "magic" from theater won't be easy.

Demystifying the classroom is of course harder, but I look for validation where I can find it. In fact, I have finally come to feel that others could help themselves by legitimating me. Others who seem *unam*-

biguously at the center could keep getting pleasure from noting that *withdrawal* can assume an infinity of *forms*, that the world offers a surfeit of unacknowledged models for creativity which are yet to be certified as meaningful parts of the curriculum. What is more, those at the center could respond to their political sensibilities and take small steps that betray awareness of their undeveloped disposition. They could engage in what R. D. Laing has called microrevolutions, movements toward no end—only toward the still hidden discipline for becoming political. They could slowly learn to perceive that refusing and withdrawing are activities and that sustaining refusals and withdrawals is demanding. They could begin to share my distrust of true scholars and able technicians who have arrived. Ceasing to build monuments and renouncing careers, they could participate in doing nothing—and keep doing so with increasing skill, tact, wit, and composure.

CHAPTER 8

Values and Evaluation in Teaching Political Science

VERNON VAN DYKE and LANE DAVIS
University of Iowa

Teachers of political science can legitimately pursue a number of objectives. We want to focus on one set of them: those pertaining to normative values (chiefly moral and jural) and to related kinds of evaluation.

We take it for granted that students in our courses are, or are likely to be, participants in politics, if only as voters; at the very least, they are interested observers of politics. As participants or observers, they necessarily face political conditions and practices, and confront issues, that call for some kind of decision on their part: an appraisal, a judgment, a choice. As we see it, the major general objective of teaching should be to help students make better decisions, and the question is how to accomplish this.[1]

To help students make better decisions is to help in a potentially complex process. Moral choices may be involved—fundamental values —basic conceptions of the desirable. Distinctions may need to be made between good and evil and, for that matter, between differing conceptions of the good and differing conceptions of evil. Various things that are all good may need to be placed in an order of importance or priority, and evils may need to be ranked from the lesser to the greater. The interpretation of domestic constitutions and international charters may be involved too: not that our students need to be lawyers, but surely they need as clear a conception as possible of the meaning of such normative propositions as that free speech shall be respected, the equal protection of the laws afforded, human rights promoted, and

147

aggression forsworn. Moreover, in addition to a knowledge of moral and jural standards, students need a capacity to apply the standards in concrete circumstances, which means that they need a capacity both to make evaluations themselves and to judge the evaluations of others. The evaluations that we have in mind vary in nature. Some are frankly and openly normative, as when a judgment is made that a given policy or state of affairs is desirable. Some involve a mixture of the normative and the descriptive, and we will call them descriptive evaluations. The evaluative element in the mixed statements is usually clear when they involve judgments about interrelationships among ends, about the actual or potential consequences of using certain means or strategies, about the performance of particular actors, about the effectiveness of given institutions, and so on.[2] An evaluative element is also present, although not always so clearly, when one descriptive word or one category is selected rather than another—for example, when a government is called democratic rather than dictatorial. Some descriptive evaluations are also called perceptions or interpretations.

Given the above, we can state our central proposition more fully as follows: that the main general objective of undergraduate teaching in political science should be to help the student make better appraisals, judgments, and choices by helping him to (a) select, understand, and justify a series of normative beliefs, (b) acquire empirical knowledge relating to those beliefs, (c) improve his capacity to make the necessary evaluations, and (d) become more sharply aware of the evaluative element in statements that he and others make.

Substantial agreement exists in the profession on the need to promote knowledge of the empirical, but there is disagreement about the proper role of the teacher with respect to normative values and widespread neglect of normative and descriptive evaluation. That is why we choose to focus on problems relating to values and evaluation. We believe that the teaching of political science relates unavoidably to normative values and unavoidably includes various kinds of evaluation; moreover, we believe that deliberate teaching about values and evaluations is desirable, and that it should be undertaken as a major part of the teacher's job and should not be minimized or deprecated. We recognize the dangers of bias and advocacy, but we believe that greater dangers attend a neglect of values and evaluations. Further, we see various ways of reducing and controlling the dangers in the one case, but no way of doing so in the other.

Normative Values

That teachers of political science should give attention to normative values, both moral and jural, seems obvious to us. Morality and law are basic to the political life of the United States and of the world, and they are basic to the appraisals, judgments, and choices that political actors and political observers make. Questions about morality and law are always arising. What kinds of conditions and practices should be considered just?[3] What is the meaning of the statement that all men are created equal, and how does equality relate to justice? If men are endowed with inalienable rights, what are those rights? What is meant by the consent of the governed? What are the justifications for attributing dignity and worth to the individual person, and what are the implications for constitutions, laws, and governmental practices? If nations are entitled to be states, are they (and are other kinds of groups) entitled alternatively to special status and rights within a multinational or non-national state? Why freedom, whether for individuals or for ethnic or national groups, and what constitutes freedom? Why peace? Why obey the law? Should one oppose genocide and racism? Why? What are the arguments for and against democracy and dictatorship?

It is scarcely imaginable that any student who takes much work in political science should be left without tutelage on questions such as these. They do not stem simply from the dreams of idealists. Some of them have been at the heart of political controversy and conflict from time immemorial, and all of them relate to vital political issues of our time. The politics of individual countries and of the world have been convulsed by them. Those whose memories cover Auschwitz, the Gulag Archipelago, and Mylai—and Watergate—should have no doubt about the interrelationships of moral and political issues, nor should those who contemplate racism in the United States and South Africa, and the degradation that exists along side of wealth in this country and over the world.

We do not know with any precision or reliability how widely our view may be shared in the profession. We know that Max Weber (as interpreted by Harry Eckstein) took a view that contrasts with ours, and we suppose that the view has been influential. Weber recognized the existence of moral issues, of course, but assigned them to politicians and recommended their exclusion from the classroom. This is indicated in Harry Eckstein's summary of Weber's views.

> Since choice is the essential business of politics—choices of ultimate goals that require moral commitments and of immediate means that cannot be purely technical since they may have to be selected upon inadequate technical knowledge and may pose moral problems of their own—politicians need, and generally develop, passionate convictions and a sense of certainty, even personal infallibility. The social scientist's vocation, per contra, is morally silent. . . . The chief danger social scientists should avoid in regard to political activity is to play at being moral teachers, agitators, demagogs, and "prophets" in their professional capacities, most of all in the classroom. . . .[4]

The latter part of this statement is obviously loaded in that teaching addressed to moral issues is gratuitously associated with play rather than with serious inquiry and in that the teacher is gratuitously associated with agitators, demagogs, and prophets.

We reject the view. To be sure, a great many questions in political science lend themselves to scientific treatment, and we favor a scientific approach to them. But other questions in political science call for normative judgment, and we believe that classroom teachers should help students with the problems that they involve. We share the spirit of a statement that David Apter makes.

> . . . [P]olitical life . . . is an endless search, sometimes through violence and often in fear of it, for a moral community through which man hopes to realize his individual moral personality. . . .
>
> Having lost its religious basis, our society is in danger of becoming a system of organized plunder in which meaning derives only from personal gain, orderliness becomes mere containment of anarchy, and the concept of humanness has no wider dimension than an individual's functional value. . . . How to restore identity and solidarity is the key problem of our society.[5]

Historically, the kinds of questions to which we are pointing emerged mainly in the context of domestic politics, and many of the moral principles at issue have come to be included in domestic constitutions and laws. Especially since World War II they have come up at the international level as well. The Declaration of Philadelphia illustrates the point. The International Labor Organization adopted it in 1944 and made it a part of its constitution. The Declaration says that:

a. All human beings, irrespective of race, creed, or sex, have the right to pursue both their material well-being and their spiritual development in conditions of freedom and dignity, of economic security and equal opportunity;

b. The attainment of conditions in which this shall be possible must constitute the central aim of national and international policy;

c. All national and international policies and measures . . . should be judged in this light and accepted only in so far as they may be held to promote and not to hinder the achievement of this fundamental objective.

Similarly, the Charter of the United Nations commits the members to a number of normative principles, including the principle that human rights shall be promoted.

With governments adopting normative principles at both the national and the international level, we repeat what seems to us the obvious imperative: that these principles, together with competing and related principles, should get critical attention in the undergraduate classroom. A statement by Donald V. Smiley might be noted, made in his presidential address to the Canadian Political Science Association in 1969, that ". . . the protection of human rights is the final end of government and . . . the degree to which human rights are safeguarded is the final test by which any polity should be judged."[6]

The teaching of normative principles should of course be an intellectual enterprise and not simply an effort to inculcate certain words and phrases in the minds of students.[7] We are not making a brief for pious moralizing or ideological indoctrination. The words and phrases expressing normative principles are commonly vague. Teaching that concerns them should be designed, among other things, to explore their meaning; it should be designed to clarify, to identify and appraise various meanings, and perhaps to identify a favored meaning along with the reasons thought to justify it. Reasoned elucidation is as important in political science as explanation. It may as well be recognized that whoever clarifies and appraises the meaning of normative principles helps to shape and in a sense create them, and he is likely to influence others to accept or reject them. Further, two or more normative principles are commonly relevant to a political decision or action, which indicates a need to examine their interrelationships. Do the principles reinforce each other, or are they somehow in conflict? If they are in conflict, what considerations need to be taken into account in assigning them an order of importance or an order of priority? Again an examination of such questions in the classroom is likely to influence those involved. Moreover, the very fact that attention is given to normative principles tends to lend importance to them. These implications of teaching seem to us to be quite acceptable, given the commitment to truth and reason that we will discuss below.

It is of course traditional that the normative should be analyzed in courses on political theory and philosophy. This is as it should be, and we believe that such courses should be regarded, at the minimum, as thoroughly proper in the political science curriculum if not central to that curriculum. In addition, in our view, the normative should get some attention in other courses as well, the amount of attention varying with the course. Every course in political science derives its justification from the contribution that it makes to the good and the right, and it seems to us that the intended contribution should at least be mentioned and perhaps elaborated on. Thus students can be reminded of the importance of moral principle, and thus the significance and relevance of the course can be established.

Normative and Descriptive Evaluations

As indicated at the outset, we have several kinds of evaluation in mind. The importance of normative values clearly implies the need for moral evaluations and for evaluations relating to the general normative principles that are incorporated in domestic and international law. What we are calling descriptive evaluations are also necessary; among them are the evaluations that occur in statements concerning the interrelationships of ends and means or in the choice of one descriptive word or category rather than another.[8]

These kinds of evaluation are virtually inevitable. It is doubtful whether the discussion of ends and means can reasonably be avoided in teaching political science. Everything, or almost everything, in the curriculum deals somehow with policies at the international or domestic level, whether they are fixed in treaties, constitutions, laws, or judicial decisions, or by executive or administrative action. By their very nature policies are purposive. They reflect a selection of values, or at least a ranking of values in an order of priority. They are designed to promote or protect values. By their very nature too, policies include strategies—include a selection of means. Inevitably a number of goals are pursued simultaneously, and a number of strategies, and problems arise about them individually and about their interrelationships. If the goal is representative democracy, questions arise about who is to be represented and how this can best be arranged. If the goals include both security for the nation and liberty for the individual, questions arise about the meaning of each term, about the standards for judging what degree of security and liberty exist, and about the strategies that will maximize net goal achievement. If the goal is self-realization for individuals, a whole panoply of questions arise—questions of meaning, questions of strategy, and questions of interrelationships among strategies. All call for evaluation. They call for empirical knowledge too, to be sure. An intimate relationship exists between a capacity to explain and predict on an empirical basis and a capacity to choose strategies that maximize the achievement of goals. Our point is simply that evaluations necessarily occur.

Similarly, the choice of descriptive words and categories is inevitable, and the choice reflects evaluations. To describe a state as national rather than multi-national is to make an evaluation. To say that a foreign policy aims at security is to make an evaluation. To describe a person as a terrorist rather than a freedom fighter, or vice versa, is to make an evaluation. To speak of malapportionment is to make evaluations. To criticize or defend the seniority rule for the selection of chairmen of congressional committees is to make evaluations. Of course, a teacher may not explicitly criticize or defend the seniority rule, but may limit himself to a description of the rule and its consequences and to an analysis of the criticisms and defenses that others offer. How fully he can thus avoid making evaluations himself is a question. Even if he can substantially avoid them when he tries hard to do so, he can scarcely do it throughout his teaching, for it would be too cumbersome to avoid all the various concepts and classifications that intrinsically are evaluative.

Charles R. Nixon is the author of an article that illustrates the point—an article of high quality. It is entitled "The Conflict of Na-

tionalisms in South Africa."[9] The words *black, Bantu, African, white,*
and *European* appear frequently in the article, and inevitably they suggest color and race, but Nixon's references are not to a conflict of
races but to a conflict of nationalisms. There is a white nationalism,
especially an Afrikaner nationalism, implemented through policies of
apartheid, and the blacks are said to be inspired by a nationalism of
their own. In the whole article the words *race, racial,* and *multi-racial*
each appear only once, and the word *racism* does not appear at all.
There is no direct reference to *civil* or *human rights,* and the word
discriminatory appears only once, and then in a quotation. There is
no intimation that what is going on in South Africa might be thought
of as a struggle over issues pertaining to human equality and racial
discrimination. What Nixon does is to discuss the conflict in South
Africa in terms favored by the South African whites, especially by
the Afrikaners. The point here is not that he is wrong, but that his
very choice of words implies evaluations. It goes without saying that
when Gwendolen Carter wrote of *The Politics of Inequality* in South
Africa, she made evaluations too.[10] As Benn and Peters point out, in
certain contexts "we call a distinction an 'inequality' only when we
have already decided to condemn it."[11]

Where evaluations reflect a combination of the normative and the
empirical, it is arguable whether they should be classified as normative or descriptive. From our point of view this is not crucial. The
crucial point is that the teaching of political science necessarily requires evaluations. They are inescapable. To be sure, specific statements
can be made and specific topics can be treated in such a way that the
clearly normative evaluations of the teacher (especially his moral evaluations) play a minor role, if they are detectable at all, but this is
scarcely possible in undergraduate courses considered in their entirety.
The subjects that they cover are so general and broad that evaluations
of one or more kinds are inevitable.

The fact suggests danger. One is that teachers who are or become
sensitive to the fact of evaluations may shy away from making them
and try to exclude them from their teaching in so far as they can manage to do so. This might be the reaction of those who, after Weber,
want to emphasize the *science* of political science, and it might be the
reaction of those who want to go to great lengths to avoid inculcating
their biases. Obviously, we deplore this kind of reaction, however
commendable the motives. It serves students poorly. Given the assump-

tion that the main thing students should get out of undergraduate instruction in political science is a capacity to make better appraisals, judgments, and choices, they need to be exposed to appraisals, judgments, and choices in the classroom and in the reading that they do. Questions raised by Watergate about the moral sensitivity of those trained in law schools have potential relevance to those trained in political science.

We are glad to note that Robert A. Dahl takes a position that resembles ours. He expresses the view that "American political scientists have in recent years largely forsworn attempts to evaluate political systems in an explicit and systematic fashion," and he regrets this.

> The legacy of two millenia of formal thought about political life is rich with implicit and explicit ideas about appraising the achievements and worth of different political systems, not only abstract alternatives but concrete systems. I suggest that we deliberately milk these ideas for all they can yield directly or by suggestion in the way of criteria of value and measures of performance and design new ones wherever the old ideas are deficient; and that we apply these criteria and measures to the great flow of cross-national data in order to appraise the performance of different political systems.[12]

To refer to another contribution to the same book from which we are quoting, Edward Shils provides an example of the kind of thing we have in mind as desirable. He assigns moral value to privacy, and he examines the implications for privacy of a proposal to establish a national data center, rendering a reasoned judgment that the implications are adverse.[13]

We do not know of studies that indicate to what extent college students in political science courses now get satisfactory training relating to values and evaluations. It is interesting to note, however, that a study directed at young Americans, ages 9, 13, 17, and 26 to 35, leads to comments by Judith A. Gillespie suggesting that a need is not being met.[14] "It appears that students' political knowledge is strongest in standard factual areas. They seem to have trouble, however, in applying their knowledge to various situations and in making judgments about appropriate actions. . . . The findings seem to demonstrate that students lack training in analysis and evaluation skills."

A contrasting kind of danger also exists, as suggested earlier: that teachers will inculcate bias. Teachers generally have a persuasive and even a coercive advantage over students, and their teaching might amount to indoctrination, deliberate or not. What some teachers do may resemble what agitators, demagogs, and "prophets" do, and thus resemble the kind of thing that Weber denounced. The line between making evaluations and expressing a bias, and the line between teaching and indoctrinating, is difficult to draw, and teachers may or may not always stay on the virtuous side of the line. But the danger that teaching relating to values and evaluations might involve bias does not seem to us to justify an attempt to eliminate such teaching from the classroom any more than the danger that governmental power may corrupt justifies an attempt to eliminate it in favor of anarchy. The two solutions seem to us to be equally romantic and quixotic. The answer to the problem, as we see it, is to expect from teachers a commitment to truth and reason.

Truth and Reason

To say that teachers of political science should commit themselves to truth and reason is of course to say that they should commit themselves to normative rules. The normative rules relate to justification: the justification of all kinds of statements—descriptive, prescriptive, and normative, including statements that express appraisals, judgments, and choices. They entail standards of justification relating to both thought and action. They indicate tests that propositions must meet before they can be adopted. They require that all values and evaluations involved in teaching should be open to scrutiny, and that the teacher should see to it that many are in fact scrutinized. Among other things, the classroom should be a place where the justification of all kinds of propositions should be examined, and the unjustifiable (or perhaps simply the unjustified) should not be allowed to stand unchallenged. The elucidation of meaning is commonly necessary.

The justification of propositions takes different forms, depending on their nature. Disagreement is notorious on the question whether and how normative propositions of a moral sort can be justified. One view is that their basis is essentially emotive. Another view is that natural or divine law prescribes them. Still another view is that they can be justified in terms of the question of their interrelationships and consequences—in terms of the question whether their combined effects and implications are mutually reinforcing and desirable (which itself requires moral judgment). Those seeking to justify moral values (in whatever way) must accept the possibility that their best efforts may lead only to disagreement; but it can be a rational disagreement in the sense that the bases claimed for the propositions can be laid bare and mutually understood.[15]

If justification of a commitment to truth and reason in teaching is necessary, it can be in terms of the anticipated consequences. Such a commitment permits and calls for untrammeled intellectual inquiry wherever curiosity may lead; it provides guidance almost regardless of time and circumstance; it calls for sensitivity to and respect for logic and the weight of evidence—that is, it limits claims to those supported by good reasons; it is self-corrective, requiring the acknowledgement and renunciation of error; and it opens the way, in principle at least, to universal understanding if not to universal agreement. All of these effects and implications are naturally congenial to teachers dedicated to scholarship. In fact, one wonders whether the words *scholar* and *professor* do not themselves imply a commitment to truth and reason—whether a moral imperative is not an element in the very meaning of the words. As already noted, description may include evaluation; it may imply a normative rule.

The justification of propositions other than those in the moral category usually involves less difficulty. In the case of normative rules of a constitutional or legal sort, reasoning and reasonable persons may disagree, but again a commitment to truth and reason is a commitment to explore the bases for the judgments made and to recognize that vague rules may permit judgments that differ. What is required for the justification of evaluations with a substantial descriptive component is obvious enough that we will give the question no attention here. That a commitment to truth and reason in connection with them is an enemy of bias seems clear.

In the first instance it is of course up to the individual professor to decide what the commitment to truth and reason requires, and the record shows that his judgment is responsible in a very high proportion of cases. But the professor accepting the commitment is also accountable to others for his interpretation of it. Fanatics and dogmatists often claim to speak the voice of truth and reason too, and safeguarding measures against them may be necessary. We will comment on this possibility below.

Implications for the Teacher
and for Teaching

Growing out of the above analysis and argument are six implications for the teacher and for teaching to which we wish to call attention.

1. Domestic constitutions and international agreements provide the teacher with a set of normative principles by which political systems and processes, and the performance of all kinds of political actors, can be judged. In particular, the various international documents pertaining to human rights give a comprehensive statement of the obligations and standards that governments have set for themselves. The teacher who wishes to minimize the subjective, personal element in judgments that certain things are good or right and others bad or wrong can focus on these documents, domestic and international. At the same time, like all other statements of normative principles, these documents are themselves open to critical appraisal.

2. Elucidation and evaluation are important elements in the work of the teacher. Normative principles are commonly vague and ambiguous, permitting different interpretations and applications. One of the major tasks of the teacher is to elucidate them, taking appropriate account of the factual information relevant to their elucidation. He may end up in any of several positions—perhaps recommending one interpretation, perhaps identifying the leading interpretations, perhaps simply clarifying issues that attend the problem of interpretation. Further, situations in which normative principles apply are also commonly vague—uncertain and indeterminate in some degree—so they too must be clarified. Definitions of the situation are of course primarily descriptive, but, as we have argued above, descriptions include evaluative elements. So does the analysis of ends and means. The important thing is that both teacher and student be aware of the role that evaluations play, and that they should be watchful lest implicit evaluations occur that are unjustifiable.

3. Since we are assuming that undergraduate teaching should be concerned with appraisals, judgments, and choices, we must assume that it should be concerned with decisionmaking—with strategies of decision.[16] Studies of the subject are generally directed toward the decisionmaking of others—of governmental officials and agencies—but the principles arrived at are applicable to the personal decisions of

teachers and students. Decisionmaking is said to be synoptic, incremental, or mixed. Synoptic decisionmaking takes nothing for granted, insisting on a thorough consideration of everything that is relevant. Incremental decisionmaking takes existing rules and practices for granted, in general, insisting only on considering the case for marginal change. We are attracted to the third type, which Amitai Etzioni calls *mixed-scanning*, requiring differentiation between fundamental decisions and bit or item decisions. Fundamental decisions are ideally to be made on the basis of a modified form of the synoptic model, and within their context bit or item decisions are to be made incrementally. This fits with the belief that it is vital for students and others to have a set of fundamental normative principles which they can articulate and justify and in the light of which they can handle the lesser issues that call for judgment.[17]

4. It is manifestly imperative for teachers committed to truth and reason to be selective in the issues with which they deal. In every polity issues arise about which teachers of political science individually and collectively lack either relevant general expertise or relevant specific knowledge or both. Whether to build a municipal parking ramp and where to locate it may be a political issue; so may be the question whether to have a sales tax or what it should be, whether to construct a new highway or what its route should be, whether to elect one candidate rather than another, and even whether a person should join a political party and if so which one. It is not practicable, and it would scarcely be honest, for teachers of political science to concern themselves with all aspects of all political issues; some must be left, in whole or in part, to teachers in other disciplines, and some are so specific and particular that they are scarcely suitable for academic attention except perhaps as items in an aggregate or as illustrations. It is the more general issues and principles—the more general political thought—with which teachers should be concerned.

5. Teachers committed to truth and reason should seek to include students in that commitment, leading them in the thoughtful consideration of the problems taken up. They can do this in a variety of ways —through the reading material assigned, through special projects such as the writing of papers, through simulation exercises, and through classroom lectures and discussions. Judith Shklar describes the teaching methods of Plato and Aristotle in such a way as to suggest a good example for the undergraduate classroom. "In both each step of the

argument is defined and debated and open to further discussion in a way that is designed to shut out mere credulity. It is just this feature of public discussion, as opposed to passive acceptance, that marks rational and objective thought."[18] And Donald W. Hanson offers a prescription for political philosophers that is applicable to teachers in every field of political science: that they should adopt "a self-consciously critical perspective which involves awareness of arguments against [their views and] includes at least tacit dialogue with rival views."[19]

In many cases the teacher committed to truth and reason must conclude that they do not provide a sufficient basis for choice between rival views. His job then is to make sure that students are aware of this, and aware that a choice, if made, reflects considerations in addition to those that scholarship supports.

6. We have mentioned individual professional commitments to truth and reason as the main safeguard against the dangers of bias and advocacy. Given the nature of the training and experience of those who seek appointment as political scientists, this safeguard is normally sufficient. Nevertheless a number of additional safeguards are readily available. Probably the most obvious of them relate to the criteria employed in recruiting and in deciding on rewards in terms of rank and salary. Ideological pluralism is desirable, and deliberate efforts to assure it may in some circumstances be necessary. Fanatics should not be recruited or rewarded. Team-teaching can carry pluralism into a single course. Opportunities can be given to students to defend themselves against the ideologically dogmatic teacher, perhaps through an arrangement for the publication of course-evaluations and perhaps even through an academic ombudsman. And other safeguards are possible. We see no way to safeguard the student against the dangers associated with ignorance of values and evaluation, but many ways to safeguard him against the teacher who is overbearing in pressing his own point of view.

We believe that a concern for values and evaluation gives undergraduate teaching a significance that it can achieve in no other way. Of course, those who neglect the normative may succeed intuitively in attacking the questions that are significant and in mobilizing descriptive knowledge and empirical theories accordingly, but the structure of their thought is necessarily truncated and incomplete. A recognition of the role of values and evaluation permits an architectonic approach to teaching, giving a basis for deciding what knowledge is needed—what fits and what does not—and permitting the organization of thought and knowledge in a coherent whole.

FOOTNOTES

1. Cf., Cleo H. Cherryholmes and Paul R. Abramson, "A Normative Theory of Political Education," *Teaching Political Science*, 1 (October 1973), 7-33.

2. Cf., Eugene J. Meehan, *Contemporary Political Thought. A Critical Study* (Homewood, Ill.: Dorsey, 1967), pp. 41-43.

3. Christian Bay, "Thoughts on the Purposes of Political Science Education," in George J. Graham, Jr., and George W. Carey, eds., *The Post-Behavioral Era. Perspectives on Political Science* (New York: David McKay, 1972), pp. 88-99.

4. Harry Eckstein, "Political Science and Public Policy," in Ithiel de Sola Pool, ed., *Contemporary Political Science: Toward Empirical Theory* (New York: McGraw-Hill, 1967), pp. 148-149, 151.

5. David E. Apter, *The Politics of Modernization* (Chicago: University of Chicago Press, 1965), pp. 11, 426.

6. Donald V. Smiley, "The Case Against the Canadian Charter of Human Rights," *Canadian Journal of Political Science*, 2 (September 1969), 278.

7. Cf., Jerrold R. Coombs, "Objectives of Value Analysis," in Lawrence E. Metcalf, ed., *Values Education. Rationale, Strategies, and Procedures* (Washington: National Council for the Social Studies, 41st Yearbook, 1971), pp. 1-28.

8. Cf., Fred M. Frohock, *Normative Political Theory* (Englewood Cliffs, N.J.: Prentice-Hall, 1974), pp. 15-18.

9. Charles R. Nixon, "The Conflict of Nationalisms in South Africa," *World Politics*, 11 (October 1958), 44-67.

10. Gwendolen M. Carter, *The Politics of Inequality. South Africa Since 1948* (New York: Praeger, 1958).

11. S. I. Benn and R. S. Peters, *The Principles of Political Thought. Social Foundations of the Democratic State* (New York: Free Press, 1965), p. 136.

12. Robert A. Dahl, "The Evaluation of Political Systems," in Pool, *op. cit.*, pp. 167, 170.

13. Edward Shils, "Privacy and Power," in Pool, *op. cit.*, pp. 231-276.

14. *DEA News*, Spring-Summer, 1974, p. 1.

15. Hanna Fenichel Pitkin, *Wittgenstein and Justice* (Berkeley: University of California Press, 1972), pp. 152-154.

16. Cf., Cherryholmes and Abramson, *loc. cit.*, pp. 17-20.

17. Cf., Amitai Etzioni, *The Active Society. A Theory of Societal and Political Processes* (New York: Free Press, 1968), esp. pp. 282-295. Edward I. Friedland, *Introduction to the Concept of Rationality in Political Science*. University Programs Modular Studies (Morristown, N.J.: General Learning Press, 1974).

18. Judith N. Shklar, "Facing Up to Intellectual Pluralism," in David Spitz, ed., *Political Theory and Social Change* (New York: Atherton, 1967), p. 281.

19. Donald W. Hanson, "The Nature of Political Philosophy: Ideas, Argument, and the Necessity of Choice," in Donald W. Hanson and Robert Booth Fowler, *Obligation and Dissent: An Introduction to Politics* (Boston: Little, Brown, 1971), p. xv.

CHAPTER 9

Political Science and Afro-Americans: Normative Problems of American Politics

MARTIN KILSON

Harvard University

I. Introduction

The subject matter of the field of inquiry called Afro-American Studies possesses many enriching opportunities for both research and teaching in political science. In recent years there has been a tendency to question whether this statement is valid, owing mainly to the emergence of black separatist militancy among black students and scholars in political science. The black separatists have argued that Afro-American Studies cannot be treated as a field of comparative political analysis because the modernizing experience of Negroes in American society has very little in common with that of other ethnic groups or subsystems.[1] Instead, it is argued that Afro-American modernization is to be understood, as it were, *on its own terms*.

A few critical comments on this issue will be sufficient to dismiss it. First, the claim for the historical uniqueness of the Afro-American experience is little more than a latter-day variant of the outmoded ethnocentric approaches to history and the social sciences (what Robert Merton characterizes as the "Insider" vs. "Outsider" dispute) that prevailed before World War II.[2] Second, the spokesmen for the historical uniqueness of the Afro-American subsystem are for the most part ignorant of the extensive scholarship—undertaken in the first half of this century—which actually treats the Afro-American experience largely *on its own terms*. This primitive stage in the development of Afro-American Studies is long past. It is now necessary to enter the more sophisticated stage of the comparative analysis of the Afro-American subsystem.[3] The need to understand this subsystem for both theoretical and practical purposes is too important to allow the sacrifice of Afro-American Studies on the altar of black separatist politics.

In what ways, then, can Afro-American Studies prove enriching and illuminating to the teaching of political science? Two key areas in which the Afro-American political experience enhances the teaching of political science can be delineated: 1) primacy of subsystems; 2) hypocrisy of power.

II. Primacy of Subsystems

Although the importance of subsystems (e.g., business interests, unions, professional associations, ethnic groups) for the study and teaching of political science has hardly escaped recognition, it has not been adequately recognized that the Afro-American subsystem possesses much utility in this regard. The numerous structural weaknesses associated with the mobilization of Negroes into the American political process since the late nineteenth century have rendered the Afro-American subsystem a special sector of American politics. Thus the use of the Afro-American subsystem as a case study in comparative political analysis can be enormously illuminating.

Insofar as the Afro-American subsystem differs from other ethnic subsystems because of the fact that it has been and remains *a developing or modernizing subsystem*,[4] its unique status in American politics can be delineated through an analysis of the dynamics of political institutionalization and political segmentation.

Political institutionalization is essentially a question of political order. By *political order* I mean something more than the maintenance of peace. Political order is, in its modernizing dimension, a matter of creating political relations and modalities that are capable of mediating conflicting interests in a manner that does not impede the modernizing (power-creating) functions of other social relations.[5] Thus political institutionalization is primarily a "boundary problem"—a problem of pragmatically delimiting the secular and sacred constituents of political relationships and interactions.[6] The political institutionalization of Negroes and their subsystem has displayed, until recently, a special set of problems in this regard, owing to what might be called the *ultra-stigmatization* of Negroes in American life—racism if you will.

Why does the *ultra-stigmatization* of Negroes in American life truncate the political institutionalization of the Afro-American subsystem? *Ultra-stigmatization* is essentially a *sacred* (atavistic) behavioral category; it is mystical and mythical, and like all forms of primordial group perception (e.g., tribalism in Africa) it defies rationalization, or rather is extremely difficult to rationalize.[7] Thus efforts by Negroes to convert the socio-economic indices of modernization—that is, upward mobility—into *power equivalents* are not perceived by whites—and thus by the dominant political processes—merely as *secular* acts. Instead, *ultrastigmatization* endows such endeavors to institutionalize the Afro-American subsystem with special qualities, unnatural and demonic. Thus black efforts at political institutionalization are translated in the perceptions of whites, into sacred phenomena, facilitating on the part of whites a foreclosure conception of Afro-American institutionalization (that is, the viewpoint that any degree of black institutionalization forecloses institutionalization opportunities for whites).[8]

Political science courses that deal with cleavages can also be broadened in their analytical perspective by drawing upon the Afro-American subsystem's experience with political segmentation. This can be illustrated by an analysis of the recent changes in the segmentation dimensions of the Afro-American subsystem.

These changes have been perplexing in their highly paradoxical (dialectical) quality. A militant black group consciousness or a black ethnocentric revitalization—highly anti-systemic in form but ultimately system-reinforcing in substance—has been the main instrument used by Negroes to redefine their weak institutionalization in American politics.[9] On the one hand, this thrust for greater political institutionalization requires a strident black-white polarization, for the mobilization of Negroes into a greater power-mustering capacity is virtually inconceivable otherwise. On the other hand, as black ethnocentric mobilization realizes the benefits or payoffs from a greater power-mustering capacity, continued attachment to such mobilization becomes ambivalent. Thus during the main period of the maturation of black ethnocentric revitalization the proportion of Negroes preferring housing in racially mixed neighborhoods increased from 64% in 1963 to 74% in 1969.[10] A similar situation prevails for another basic area in black-white relationships—the job milieu. Negro preference for a racially mixed job milieu increased from 76% to 82% between 1963 and 1969, and the middle-class preference (86%) is somewhat stronger than the total black preference—a significant fact in view of the disproportionate role of the Negro middle-class in the movement of black ethnocentric mobilization.[11] Viewed from another set of data, in 1969 some 59% of Negroes disagreed with the statement that "Negroes can get what they want only by banding together as black people against the whites, because the whites will never help Negroes." Yet in the same year only 27% of Negroes felt that whites wished a "better break" for blacks.[12]

Why the ambivalence in the Negro perception of black-white cleavages suggested by these data? The key to this ambivalence is that black ethnocentric revitalization occurs within a framework *not of rigid socio-political constraints upon Negroes but of steady modification of the historic parameters dividing blacks and whites in American life.* For example, the proportion of Negroes who are poor declined in the decade of the 1960s; and blacks in white-collar and craftsmen-cum-skilled occupations increased 76% in the same period, from 2.9 million in 1960 to 5.1 million in 1970, compared to 24% increase for whites—41.6% to 57%. These occupational changes are associated with a major educational advance: median school years completed for Negroes aged 25-29 increased from 7 years in 1940 to 12 years in 1970; 10% of Negroes aged 18-24 were enrolled in college in 1965 (26% whites) and 18% in 1971 (27% whites), and the differential or gap is now only 9%.[13]

In short, it seems that despite nearly a decade of intense black-white polarization consequent to the movement of black ethnocentric revitalization, this cleavage is not perfectly continuous at the institutional level. And a significant proportion of blacks do not wish it otherwise. This is suggested by data on black attitudes for the period from 1969 to late 1972, which show a sharp decline in blacks' perception of discrimination in numerous areas of black-white interactions. For example, there is a 17-point decline in Negroes' perception of housing discrimination—from 83% in 1969 to 66% in late (December) 1972.[14]

Thus it appears that as black ethnocentric mobilization achieves benefits for Negroes, the pluralistic inclusionary pressures of American society function as a counterweight to the long-run polarization of blacks and whites. This tendency toward a pluralistic inclusionary equilibrium is found in other historic areas of conflict in America society, as Robert Dahl demonstrates in regard to ethnic-class cleavages in twentieth century New Haven between lower-class Catholics, on the one hand, and patrician WASPs, on other.[15] The Afro-American subsystem's experience with cleavages provides equally fascinating analytical perspectives for teaching political science courses that deal with segmentation dynamics.

III. Hypocrisy of Power and Political Normlessness

The teaching of political science in American colleges has never adequately come to grips with the *hypocrisy of power* in American society. *This dimension of American politics is essentially a problem of normlessness—a problem of pervasive deviation by political actors from the reputed norms of the political system.* Of course, no society of flesh-and-blood human beings will ever achieve a direct correspondence between political behavior and norms, for human beings are existentially incapable of such perfection. So the problem of a gap between political behavior and norms—hereafter called the "norm gap"— is a relative issue, which of course makes it all the more fascinating and perplexing as a problem for analysis.

In American politics, the norm gap assumes numerous forms. It ranges from patent corruption and malfeasance, on the one hand, to disregard (sometimes quiet, sometimes not) of the codes of civility and fair play—the unwritten criteria of order and reciprocity (of political morality) in a society of laws—on the other hand. Political science scholarship has not of course neglected the former (although it figures little in the theoretical endeavors to understand the nature of American politics) but the latter wants for serious consideration.[16] This is pressingly so in today's world—a world infested with normlessness in political interactions and behavior, ranging from the open normlessness of Arab terrorism or Israeli counterterrorism, on the one hand, to the quiet normlessness of Watergate, on the other.

What the experience of the Afro-American subsystem has to offer political science in this regard is a veritable laboratory in which to deepen our understanding of the hypocrisy of power—normlessness and the failure of political morality—in a major modern political culture. It is an extraordinary feature of the studies of the political status of Negroes in the South prior to the 1960s that virtually none of them —including the best—grappled with the problem of the norm gap. Faithful to a vulgarized version of the pragmatic tradition in American political science, the authors of these studies simply neglected the norm gap.

At the most general level of statement, the crux of the norm gap in regard to the Afro-American subsystem during the first half of this century (during which over 60% of Negroes remained in the South) is that a modern political system based upon democratic forms pos-

sessed within the very core of its operation a thoroughgoing authoritarian tributary—the white supremacist and one-party South. Until
recently, few political scientists have seized the opportunity this situation provides for introducing more boldly into political science the
understanding *that politics is above all a question of morality. And
this, of course, is especially the case for the politics of democratic
societies: for the ultimate justification of the value of democracy over
authoritarianism must be that the former permits the realization of
a higher civility (a more enduring higher morality) in human relationships.*

Thus ever since my undergraduate days in the early 1950s at one
of the Negro colleges—Lincoln University, where my political science
teachers were John Aubrey Davis, now at CUNY, and Martin Landau,
now at University of California, Berkeley—I always had a certain un-
easiness when reading the late V. O. Key's classic study of the one-
party South, *Southern Politics in State and Nation.* Nowhere in this
seminal work is it ever apparent that Key grasped the ultimate existential character of Southern politics: that underlying what he analyzed as the intricate modalities of balancing-off the one-party politics
of the South with the competitive politics of the nation was a norm
gap of great moral gravity. To treat this norm gap, as Key did, merely
as an *incidental variable* is to contribute to the vulgarization of the
pragmatic-consensus tradition in the American political culture and
process—a vulgarization which has been aided and abetted by the past
two generations of political scientists and now running riot.

I say "vulgarization of the pragmatic-consensus tradition" because
to conceive of or evaluate the stability-creating dynamic of a political
system merely in terms of its power outcomes is tantamount to saying that political systems, like human beings, "live by bread (power)
alone." But this was at best a dubious claim by the time V. O. Key
researched *Southern Politics in State and Nation* (with the Fascist and
Communist experience hanging over his generation of political scientists) and is hardly worthy of serious debate in today's world. In
short, the Afro-American subsystem provides political scientists with
a rare opportunity to extend their concern to the ultimate issues inherent in all politics—the issues of morality, of ultimate purposes, and
of the larger meanings of those regulated human choices concerned
with the production of goods and services in civilized society.

For the American political process as such, it is not too much to say that the deep-seated and pervasive normlessness surrounding the authoritarian status of the Afro-American subsystem in the South throughout the late nineteenth century and for 60 years of this century functioned within the total system *as a morally malignant force, providing justification for normlessness in other regions and at all levels of the system.*[17] There is no more important task confronting American political scientists today than to grasp the significance of this for understanding today's massive crisis of morality in American politics, and in other institutions as well.

Using the Afro-American political experience as an impetus to restore the place of morality in the teaching of political science to today's generation of students does not mean, however, that one should embark upon a moralistic crusade. I dislike crusades. Nor is it meant to suggest that Afro-Americans themselves possess, by virtue of their experience with authoritarian constraints in a democratic polity, an intrinsic capacity to inform American political life with a higher morality.

Indeed, there is no blueprint for ensuring a greater civility and human sensitivity in American politics—or in any other political system. Civility and human sensitivity in politics are, I am afraid, essentially situational in character. They exist because political relations and interactions are structured in ways that are conducive to civility. What our discipline needs, therefore, is *a political science of civility—a subfield of political science inquiry which analyzes political processes in terms of how they are conducive to or destructive of civility, a higher morality in power relationships.* The political status of Afro-Americans, characterized by extraordinary discrepancy between the norms and practice of American democracy, is especially ideal as an area for such inquiry.

IV. Concluding Note: A Political Science of Civility

What is a political science of civility? Until this subfield of political inquiry gains greater specification, the answer to this question should be derived from a given political system. Robert Merton's distinction between the manifest and latent functions of American city machines provides a starting point for a conceptualization of a political science of civility.[18] This distinction suggests two things about political structures: first, the manifest functions are not necessarily the most significant, for unintended or latent functions inherent in political structures might ultimately prove more salient; second, the latent functions are not necessarily supportive of the manifest functions and their long-run purposes.[19]

That aspect of the gap between manifest and latent functions wherein the latter prove non-supportive of the former is, I think, a primary sphere of analysis for a political science of civility. Both the cause of political normlessness and the sources of civility are located somewhere in the dynamics associated with this gap. Why is this so?

First, the discrepancy between manifest and latent functions is essentially (although not solely) a matter of morality or norms. Men deviate from the manifest functions of political forms and processes because 1) they do not fully share the principles and ideals (the normative underpinnings) which inform those political processes, or because 2) their interests are perceived as threatened by adherence to the normative substructure, causing either neutrality toward it or outright deviation. Whether the first or second situation is the cause of incongruity between the manifest and latent functions of political forms is a vital aspect of the primary sphere of analysis for a political science of civility.

In both of these conditions of deviation from the manifest functions of political processes, the issue of socialization would seem salient. Thus a second area of analysis for a political science of civility is that of political socialization. Both the sources of *variation in socialization to the normative substructure of a political system* and the nature of the *conflict-threshold of commitment to a normative substructure* are central problems for a political science of civility. In many ways they are, in fact, *the* central problems for analysis for they are both logically and factually prior to the problem of incongruity between manifest and latent functions—that is, the failure of the latter to reinforce the former. Most political actors experience an important measure of political socialization before they partake of politics, and this socialization is in turn a crucial element in their conception of what I call the conflict-threshold of normative commitment.

Finally, our conception of a political science of civility has special applicability to the problems of normlessness in regard to the Afro-American political experience. The character of the stigma applied to Negroes by white racism renders their political status vulnerable to white behavior that deviates from the normative substructure of

American politics. This, in turn, makes it difficult for even the manifest functions of this politics to assert themselves in regard to blacks, let alone to facilitate congruity between the manifest and latent functions. Thus we can derive from this a major hypothesis for a political science of civility: Where the sacred (atavistic) perception of political relationships supersedes the secular perception, those relationships will display a high degree of normlessness; and, conversely, where the secular (interest-related) perception supersedes the sacred, political relationships will exhibit a low degree and/or a politically manageable form of normlessness.

Thus a major goal of a political science of civility is to prescribe how atavistic perceptions of political relationships can be minimized through socialization processes (including the teaching of political science) and structural renovations. Surely this goal should be high on the list of those political scientists who are concerned with the issue of the teacher and the polity.

FOOTNOTES

1. See, e.g., the chapter by Houston Baker in Nathan I. Huggins, Martin Kilson, and Daniel M. Fox, eds., *Key Issues in the Afro-American Experience* (New York: Harcourt Brace Jovanovich, 1971-), Vol. I.

2. See Robert K. Merton, "Insiders and Outsiders: A Chapter in the Sociology of Knowledge," *American Journal of Sociology,* 78 (July, 1972), 9-47.

3. I attempt this in Martin Kilson, *Political Dilemma of Black Mayors—A Study of Carl Stokes' Mayoralty in Cleveland* (Washington, D.C.: Joint Center for Political Studies, forthcoming).

4. Development or modernization is, as Lucian Pye would say, essentially a process of realizing a greater capacity both to create and to allocate power. Cf., Lucian Pye, *Aspects of Political Development* (Boston: Little, Brown, 1966).

5. Cf., Samuel P. Huntington, *Political Order in Changing Societes* (New Haven: Yale University Press, 1968), pp. 20ff, *passim.*

6. Cf., Gabriel A. Almond and James S. Coleman, eds., *The Politics of the Developing Areas* (Princeton: Princeton University Press, 1960).

7. See Gordon W. Allport, *The Nature of Prejudice* (Cambridge: Addison-Wesley, 1954).

8. This is treated more fully in Kilson, *Political Dilemma of Black Mayors,* cited above.

9. For a fuller treatment of this, see Martin Kilson, "Blacks and Neo-Ethnicity in American Political Life," in Nathan Glazer and Daniel P. Moynihan, eds., *Ethnicity, Theory and Experience* (Cambridge: Harvard University Press, 1975), pp. 236-266.

10. Peter Goldman, *Report from Black America* (New York: Simon and Schuster, 1970), p. 179.

11. *Ibid.*, pp. 266-267.

12. *Ibid.*, pp. 260, 250.

13. Ben J. Wattenberg and Richard M. Scammon, "Black Progress and Liberal Rhetoric," *Commentary*, 55 (April, 1973), 35-44.

14. *The Harris Survey* (December, 1972).

15. Robert A. Dahl, *Who Governs? Democracy and Power in an American City* (New Haven: Yale University Press, 1961). I develop this notion of "pluralistic inclusionary pressures," the groundwork of consensus in American political culture, in Martin Kilson, *Politics and Race in American Life* (forthcoming, St. Martin's Press).

16. For an example of studies of corruption, see H. Hubert Wilson, *Congress: Corruption and Compromise* (New York: Rinehart, 1951).

17. For the normlessness associated with the authoritarian status of the blacks in the South, see Gunnar Myrdal, *An American Dilemma: the Negro Problem and Modern Democracy* (New York: Harper, 1944). See also Stetson Kennedy, *Southern Exposure* (Garden City, N.Y.: Doubleday, 1946).

18. See Robert K. Merton, *Social Theory and Social Structure* (Glencoe: Free Press, 1949, 1968).

19. This feature of the manifest-latent function dynamic is implied in Merton's formulation but not fully developed.

About the Contributors

Peter Bachrach
> Ph.D., Harvard University, 1952. Political philosophy. Temple University, 1968-. Bryn Mawr College, 1952-68. Rockefeller Foundation Fellow, 1957-58, 1964-65. Award for distinguished teaching, Temple University, 1970. Nominee of the Caucus for a New Political Science for President of the American Political Science Association, 1972 and 1973. *Power and Choice: The Formulation of American Population Policy* (with Eli Bergman; 1973). The *Role of Political Elites in a Democracy* (1971). *Power and Poverty* (with Morton Baratz, 1970). *Theory of Democratic Elitism* (1967).

Douglas C. Bennett
> Ph.D., Yale University, 1976. Political philosophy. Temple University, 1973-. Social Science Research Council Fellow, 1975-76. "Obstacles to Graduate Education in Political Science" (co-author), *P.S.*, Fall, 1969. Offers a course on the teaching of political science.

Allan Bloom
> Ph.D., University of Chicago, 1955. Political philosophy. University of Toronto, 1970-. Cornell University, 1962-1970. Guggenheim Fellow, 1975-76. Rockefeller Fellow, 1957-58. *The Education of Democratic Man: Rousseau's Emile* (forthcoming, 1977). *Plato's Republic* (tr., notes, interpretative essay; 1968). *Shakespeare's Politics* (with Harry V. Jaffa; 1964). Rousseau's *Politics and the Arts: Letter to d'Alembert on the Theatre* (tr., notes, introduction; 1960).

Lane Davis
> Ph.D., Cornell University, 1950. Political theory. University of Iowa, 1949-. "British Socialism and the Perils of Success," *Political Science Quarterly*, December 1954. "The Cost of Realism: Contemporary Restatements of Democracy," *Western Political Quarterly*, March 1964.

Martin Diamond
> Ph.D., University of Chicago, 1956. Political philosophy. Northern Illinois University, 1972-. Claremont Men's College, 1958-71.

173

Fellow, National Institute for the Humanities, Yale University, 1975-76. Fellow, Woodrow Wilson International Center for Scholars, 1974-75. Earhart Fellow, 1966-67. Rockefeller Fellow, 1963-64. Fellow, Center for the Advanced Study of the Behavioral Sciences, 1960-61. *The Democratic Republic, An Introduction to American National Government* (with Winston Mills Fisk and Herbert Garfinkel; 1966). "The Revolution of Sober Expectations," American Enterprise Institute's Distinguished Lecture Series. "The Declaration and the Constitution: Liberty, Democracy, and the Founders," *Public Interest*, Fall 1975.

Heinz Eulau

Ph.D., University of California, Berkeley, 1941. Political representation and behavior. Stanford University, 1958-. Antioch College, 1947-58. President, American Political Science Association, 1971-72. Fellow, American Academy of Arts and Sciences. Fellow, Center for Advanced Study in the Behavioral Sciences, 1957-58. Fellow, Social Science Research Council, 1956-57. Ford Foundation Fellow, 1951-52. *Labyrinths of Democracy: Adaptations, Linkages, Representation, and Policies in Urban Politics* (with Kenneth Prewitt; 1973). *Micro-Macro Political Analysis* (1969). *The Behavioral Persuasion in Politics* (1963). *The Legislative System: Explorations in Legislative Behavior* (with John C. Wahlke and others; 1962). *Class and Party in the Eisenhower Years* (1962).

Henry S. Kariel

Ph.D., University of California (Berkeley), 1954. Political theory. University of Hawaii, 1964-. Harvard University, 1955-58. Bennington College, 1958-64. *Beyond Liberalism, Where Relations Grow* (1976). *Saving Appearances: The Re-establishment of Political Science* (1972). *Open Systems: Arenas for Political Action* (1969). *The Promise of Politics* (1966). *In Search of Authority* (1964). *The Decline of American Pluralism* (1961).

Martin Kilson

Ph.D., Harvard University, 1959. Comparative politics. Harvard University, 1965-. Research Fellow, Harvard Center for International Affairs, 1961-1972. Member of Council, National Endowment for the Humanities. Fellow, American Academy of Arts and Science. Guggenheim Fellow, 1975-76. Ford Foundation Foreign Area Training Fellowship, West Africa, 1959-1961. *The Political Dilemma of Black Mayors* (forthcoming, 1977). *The African*

Diaspora (co-editor; 1976). *New States in the Modern World* (editor; 1975). *Political Change in a West African State* (1966).
Martin Landau
Ph.D., New York University, 1952. Public administration. Epistemology. University of California (Berkeley), 1972-. Brooklyn College, 1953-72. Chairman, Editorial Board, *P.S.*, 1972-74. Guggenheim Fellow and Fellow, Center for Advanced Study in the Behavioral Sciences, 1976-77. William E. Mosher Award for Distinguished Scholarship, 1970. E. Harris Harbison Award for Gifted Teaching, 1970. Distinguished Teaching Award, Brooklyn College, 1963. *Political Theory and Political Science, Studies in the Methodology of Political Inquiry* (1972).
Stanley Rothman
Ph.D., Harvard University, 1958. Comparative government. Smith College, 1964-. Ford Foundation Foreign Area Training Fellowship, 1962-63. *The Radical Impulse in Europe and America* (forthcoming, 1978). *European Society and Politics* (rev. ed., 1976). *Through Different Eyes, Black and White Perspectives on American Race Relations* (with Peter I. Rose; 1973). Expects to expand his contribution to this volume into a full-scale study of the state of contemporary political science.
Vernon Van Dyke
Ph.D., University of Chicago, 1937. International Relations/Human Rights. University of Iowa, 1949-. President, International Studies Association and Midwest Political Science Association, 1966-67. Fellow, National Endowment for the Humanities and Woodrow Wilson International Center for Scholars, 1972-73. Fellow, Social Science Research Council, 1962-63. *International Politics* (rev. ed., 1972). *Human Rights, the United States and World Community* (1970). *Pride and Power, The Rationale of the Space Program* (1964). *Political Science, A Philosophical Analysis* (1960).

INDEX

177